Microsoft Azure Network Security

Nicholas DiCola
Anthony Roman

Microsoft Azure Network Security

Published with the authorization of Microsoft Corporation by Pearson Education, Inc.

ISBN-13: 978-0-13-725204-6
ISBN-10: 0-13-725204-8

Library of Congress Control Number: 2021933677

1 2021

TRADEMARKS

WARNING AND DISCLAIMER

SPECIAL SALES

For information about buying this title in bulk quantities, or for special sales opportunities (which may include electronic versions; custom cover designs; and content particular to your business, training goals, marketing focus, or branding interests), please contact our corporate sales department at corpsales@pearsoned.com or(800) 382-3419.

For government sales inquiries, please contact governmentsales@pearsoned.com.

For questions about sales outside the U.S., please contact intlcs@pearson.com.

EDITOR-IN-CHIEF
Brett Bartow

EXECUTIVE EDITOR
Loretta Yates

SPONSORING EDITOR
Charvi Arora

DEVELOPMENT EDITOR
Songlin Qiu

MANAGING EDITOR
Sandra Schroeder

SENIOR PROJECT EDITOR
Tracey Croom

COPY EDITOR
Charlotte Kughen

INDEXER
Cheryl Ann Lenser

PROOFREADER
Donna Mulder

TECHNICAL EDITOR
Mike Martin

EDITORIAL ASSISTANT
Cindy Teeters

COVER DESIGNER
Twist Creative, Seattle

COMPOSITOR
codeMantra

Contents at a Glance

Contents

Acknowledgments

The authors would like to thank Loretta Yates and the entire Microsoft Press/Pearson team for their support in this project, Jonathan Trull for writing the foreword, and also the Azure Network Security Engineering Team (Yair Tor, Ido Frizler, Teresa Yao), Ajeet Prakash, David Fosth, Ken Hollis, and Mark Simos.) Thanks also goes to Mike Kassis for the great work writing Chapter 8. We would also like to thank Mike Martin for reviewing this book.

Nicholas would also like to thank: My wife and children for supporting me while I worked on this book and my co-author and friend, Anthony Roman, for his hard work on this book.

Anthony would also like to thank: My wife and kids for tolerating groggy mornings after late nights spent working on these chapters. Thanks to Nicholas for suggesting this project and holding me to deadlines.

About the authors

Nicholas DiCola

Nicholas is the principal director of the Cloud Security Customer Experience Engineering (CxE) team. CxE helps customers with deployments of Cloud Security products such as Azure Security Center, Azure Sentinel, Azure Network Security, Azure Information Protection, Microsoft Defender for Identities, and Microsoft Cloud Application Security. CxE is responsible for driving use of Cloud Security products and taking feedback from customers to improve the products. Nicholas has been with Microsoft since 2006 when he started in Microsoft Consulting Services. He has a Master of Business Administration with a concentration in information systems and various industry certifications such as CISSP and CEH. You can follow Nicholas on Twitter at @mastersecjedi.

Anthony Roman

Anthony is the senior PM manager leading the Azure network security Get-To-Production team within Cloud Security CxE. The team works with customers and network security engineering to ensure that products are fulfilling customer security requirements. Anthony joined Microsoft in 2019 and has held positions in IT and security since he made the transition from bartender to IT security professional a decade earlier. His Bachelor of Arts degree in philosophy is complemented by several industry certifications and plenty of on-the-job and home lab experience. He currently lives in Philadelphia with his wife and two children and can often be seen walking around the city in search of parks and restaurants.

Foreword

I am writing this foreword amid one of the largest and most invasive cybersecurity breaches in history—Solorigate. A sophisticated, nation-state actor was able to infiltrate a well-known supplier of network monitoring and management solutions. The threat actor injected a backdoor into the supplier's build system, and the backdoor was then signed with a valid certificate and pushed to approximately 18,000 customers. What made this attack particularly novel was the fact that the threat actor leveraged their access to on-premises systems to then pivot and begin accessing cloud services, which appeared to be their primary target. The attacker also attempted to hide their level of access by leveraging Azure Service Principals to blend in with standard traffic and access patterns.

With attacks like Solorigate, it is essential to have a strong understanding of how to properly segment, protect, and monitor your cloud estate. Microsoft Azure is one of the dominant public clouds available in the market today and is used extensively by both governments and commercial enterprises. Microsoft Azure offers hundreds of different cloud computing solutions to organizations that allow them to innovate quickly, increase the digital experiences for customers and employees, and reduce large outlays in capital for data centers and hardware.

While cloud computing offers amazing benefits, it also introduces risks that security and IT teams must properly manage. In this book, Nicholas and Anthony cover the foundational security services and design patterns that organizations should adopt to protect and monitor their Azure workloads. I can think of no more qualified individuals than Nicholas and Anthony to provide practical, real-world implementation guidance regarding the design of secure Azure networking architectures. From preventing volumetric DDoS attacks to monitoring security logs with Azure Sentinel, this book covers everything you need to jump-start your journey into Azure security architecture and engineering.

For every IT leader using Microsoft Azure, put this on your team's required reading list!

We are in the fight to deter cyberattacks together, and I applaud the effort that Nicholas and Anthony have put into making this essential material accessible to a broader audience. For all those who are working tirelessly to protect your organizations' data and computer systems, thank you! Look after yourselves and each other.

—Jonathan C. Trull

Introduction

Welcome to *Microsoft Azure Network Security*, a book that is intended to provide detailed information about the capabilities of the major network security components of Azure along with recommendations for how to put them all together. We pay the closest attention to what we consider the core network security resources: Azure Firewall, Azure WAF, and Azure DDoS Protection Standard. Going beyond the function of the network security components themselves, we also emphasize the value of logging and integration with other security services like Azure Sentinel.

We wrote this book from a vantage point inside Engineering at Microsoft, working closely with both the product groups in control of the development of the technology and with customers who implement the technology in their networks. Network security is a complex intersection of networking, security, and cloud operations, and our hope is that we have covered the important pieces of all of these.

This book was finished just before the public release of Azure Firewall Premium, so details are as complete as possible. Please expect the product to evolve over time.

Who is this book for?

Microsoft Azure Network Security is for anyone who has a technical role that involves Azure deployments. Cloud administrators, engineers, and architects will find value in the how-to implementation details. Networking teams can gain context for how to integrate Azure native services into the broader architecture. Security professionals will be able to use this book as a guide for both secure Azure network architecture and network security monitoring strategy.

How is this book organized?

This book is arranged into nine chapters, which represent some broad themes:

- Chapters 1 and 2 discuss the broad theme of cloud network security and introduce the Azure components that address it.
- Chapters 3, 4, 5, and 6 concentrate on the core Azure network security resources: Azure Firewall, Azure WAF, and Azure DDoS Protection Standard.

- Chapters 7 and 8 address logging, monitoring, and integration with other Azure security components such as Azure Sentinel and Security Center.
- Chapter 9 brings everything together to connect the concepts of secure network architecture and security monitoring as they apply to all the Azure network security tools.

Errata, updates, & book support

We've made every effort to ensure the accuracy of this book and its companion content. You can access updates to this book—in the form of a list of submitted errata and their related corrections—at:

MicrosoftPressStore.com/AzureNetworkSecurity/errata

If you discover an error that is not already listed, please submit it to us at the same page.

For additional book support and information, please visit *MicrosoftPressStore. com/Support*.

Please note that product support for Microsoft software and hardware is not offered through the previous addresses. For help with Microsoft software or hardware, go to *http://support.microsoft.com*.

Stay in touch

Let's keep the conversation going! We're on Twitter: http://twitter.com/MicrosoftPress.

## Chapter 1

Introduction to Azure Network Security

I n this book, we dive into the components and services that Azure provides for creating a secure network infrastructure. Before doing that, it is important that we cover some topics related to network connectivity in Azure and consider current threats and challenges when leveraging the available network security services.

The cloud allows you to create services quickly and easily, and by design, those services are exposed to the internet when created. An example is a virtual machine (VM)—when you create one, it's exposed to the internet via RDP (Remote Desktop Protocol) and SSH (Secure Shell) using the default wizard. This is done so that you can then access the VM to manage it, but attackers can access it, too. Attackers scan Azure IP ranges, which are publicly documented, and can quickly find open RDP ports to brute-force attack the VM.

This is just one example of the importance of Azure Network Security services that you need to understand and deploy to protect your environment. It's important to create a strategy and architecture that you can deploy and manage for your Azure environment to protect your applications and services.

Network connectivity

Azure provides robust network infrastructure with options and configurations that allow for simple to complex network designs. This can range from direct public access for applications that need to be accessible everywhere to private hybrid connectivity between on-prem and Azure. We cover a couple of basics of networking to set the context. We recommend you research and understand these as they are underlying to support the network security services. The following list provides a short overview of the networking services.

- **Virtual Network** A Virtual Network (VNet) is the basic building block for networks in Azure. It is similar to the local switch in traditional networks but with added benefits like scaling, high availability, and isolation. This is what VMs are attached to using virtual network interface cards (VNICs) or Platform as a Service (PaaS) when using Private Link. Figure 1-1 shows the concept of a Virtual Network.

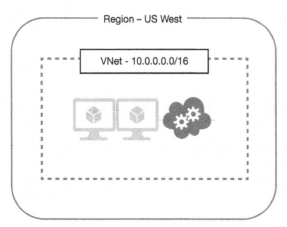

FIGURE 1-1 Basic diagram of a Virtual Network

- **VNet peering** Peering allows you to connect multiple VNets together creating one network for connectivity purposes. All the traffic between VNets is routed through Microsoft's private network only. Figure 1-2 shows multiple VNets connected with peering.

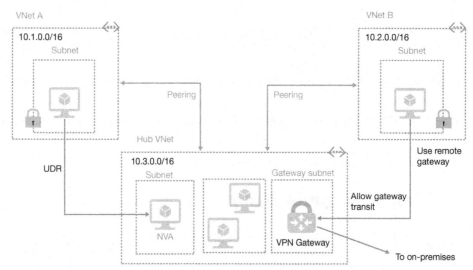

FIGURE 1-2 Basic diagram of VNet peering

- **VNet service endpoint** VNet service endpoint connects certain Azure PaaS services to a VNet over an optimized route in the Azure backbone. PaaS services are typically connected to the public internet. Service Endpoint allows VNet private IP addresses to access the PaaS service without it having a public IP. Figure 1-3 depicts the basic networking with service endpoint.

- **Private Link** Private Link allows connecting Azure PaaS services to a VNET. PaaS services are normally connected to the public internet, but with Private Link, you can give your VNets private access to the service. Figure 1-4 depicts VNets connected to a PaaS service using Private Endpoint.

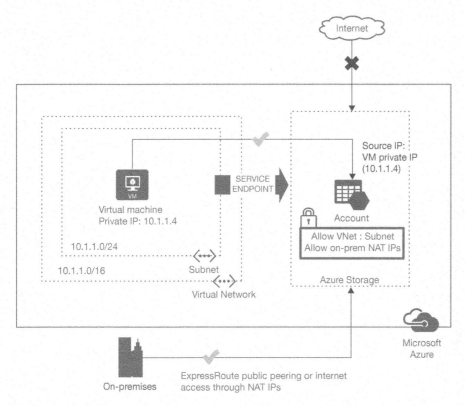

FIGURE 1-3 Basic diagram of service endpoint

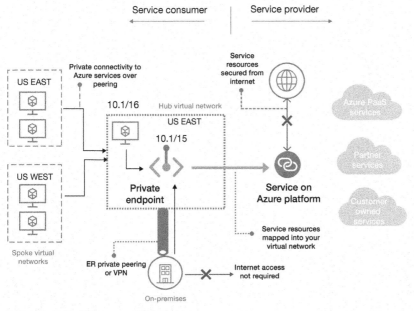

FIGURE 1-4 Basic diagram of Private Link

- **Load Balancer**   Load Balancer allows the distribution of traffic across a group of resources. It can be public or internal and operates at Layer 4 in the OSI model. Figure 1-5 shows a typical two-tier application with each tier load balanced by a Load Balancer.

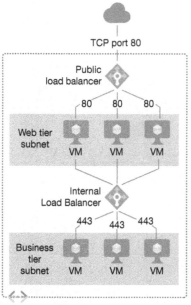

FIGURE 1-5   Basic diagram of Load Balancer

- **Traffic Manager**   Traffic Manager is a DNS-based traffic load balancer to distribute traffic across Azure regions. This allows creation of multiregion applications for reliability and redundancy, and the endpoints get routed to the application. Traffic Manager is for global deployments and can use Load Balancer in the local region behind it. Figure 1-6 shows an application in two regions with a Traffic Manager routing traffic to each region.

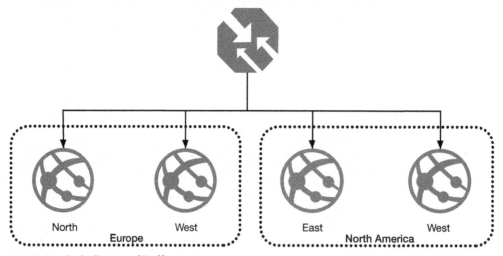

FIGURE 1-6   Basic diagram of Traffic Manager

- **Application Gateway**   Application Gateway is the step up from Load Balancer for web apps by adding layer 7 load balancing. This allows distributing traffic based on URL as an example. You can deploy a Web Application Firewall (WAF) by attaching policies to Application Gateway, which is covered in depth in Chapter 5, "Secure application delivery with Azure Web Application Firewall." Figure 1-7 shows an Application Gateway with a Web Application Firewall in-front of two different sets of VMs.

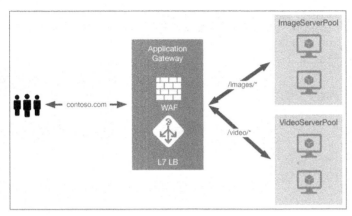

FIGURE 1-7   Basic diagram of Application Gateway

- **Front Door**   Front Door combines features from several of the preceding services to provide global routing for web applications. It can also accelerate performance by allowing users to connect to the closest Front Door Point of Presence (POP). Like Load Balancer and Traffic Manager, Front Door is the global service where Application Gateway is used for local in-region. Chapter 5 covers attaching WAF policies to Front Door as well. Figure 1-8 shows Azure Front Door in front of an active/passive application across two regions.

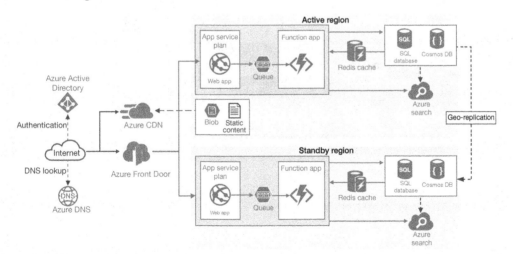

FIGURE 1-8   Basic diagram of Front Door

- **VPN Gateway**   VPN Gateway provides encrypted traffic between Azure VNets and other VNets or on-prem networks. It can be set up for point-to-site or site-to-site connectivity. Figure 1-9 depicts a basic VPN diagram using Azure VPN.

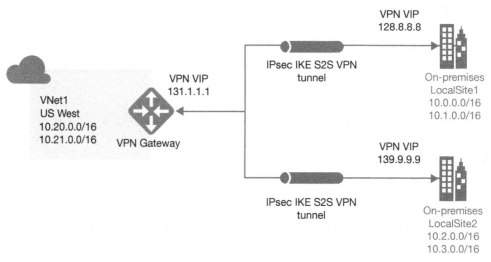

FIGURE 1-9   Basic diagram of VPN Gateway

- **ExpressRoute**   ExpressRoute can extend on-prem networks to the Microsoft cloud over a private connection. This is provided by a connectivity provider to create a private connection. Traffic over ExpressRoute does not go over the public internet. Figure 1-10 shows a diagram of ExpressRoute connections to the Microsoft cloud.

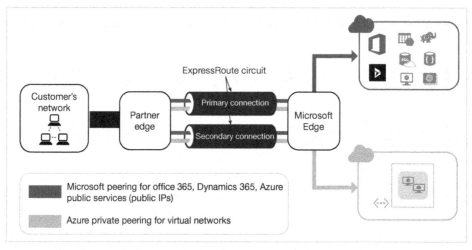

FIGURE 1-10   Basic diagram of ExpressRoute

- **Virtual WAN** Virtual WAN brings together networking, security, and routing to create a single operational interface. It includes branch connectivity, site-to-site VPN connectivity, remote user VPN connectivity, private connectivity, intracloud connectivity, VPN ExpressRoute interconnectivity, routing, Azure Firewall, and encryption for private connectivity. Figure 1-11 is a diagram of virtual WAN showing all the different types of connections it can provide.

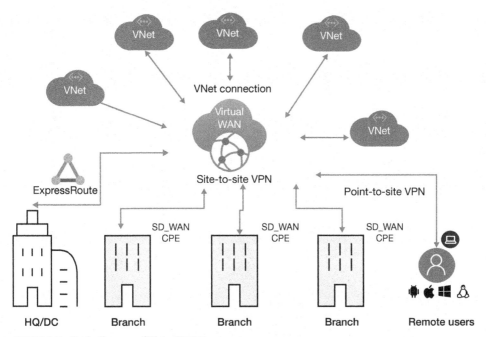

FIGURE 1-11 Basic diagram of Virtual WAN

- **Network Watcher** Network Watcher gives the ability to monitor, diagnose, enable, or disable logs and view metrics for your virtual networks. It allows you to monitor and repair the network as needed. Figure 1-12 is a dashboard from the Network Watcher service.

- **Content Delivery Network (CDN)** CDN is a global service to deliver high-bandwidth content by caching the content close to the user locations. The content is cached on edge servers in the POP. Figure 1-13 shows how CDN works where the first user request is gathered from the source and then cached for the next user.

This is not meant to be a detailed covering of the networking concepts and services in Azure, just a quick overview of the services and their purpose because it will be relevant when applying network security. Table 1-1 provides a link to detailed documentation for each of these services.

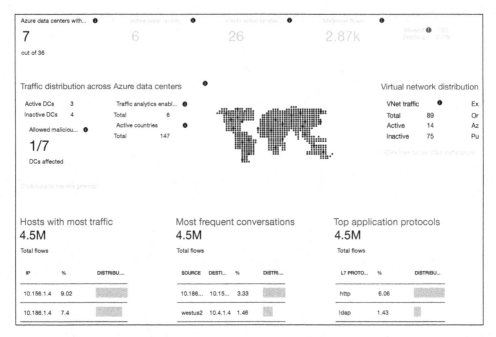

FIGURE 1-12 Network Watcher dashboard

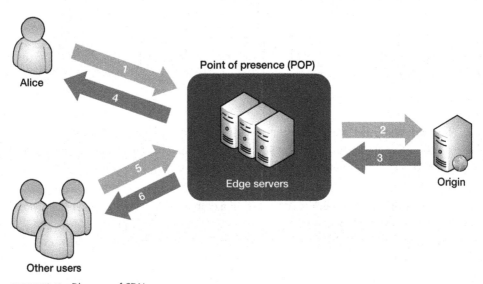

FIGURE 1-13 Diagram of CDN

TABLE 1-1 Detailed documentation for various Network Services

Network service	URL
Virtual Network	https://aka.ms/ASNSBook/VNet
VNet Peering	https://aka.ms/AzNSBook/Peering

Network service	URL
VNet Service Endpoint	https://aka.ms/AzNSBook/ServiceEndpoint
Private Link	https://aka.ms/AzNSBook/PrivateLink
Load Balancer	https://aka.ms/AzNSBook/LoadBalancer
Traffic Manager	https://aka.ms/AzNSBook/TrafficManager
Application Gateway	https://aka.ms/AzNSBook/ApplicationGateway
Front Door	https://aka.ms/AzNSBook/FrontDoor
VPN Gateway	https://aka.ms/AzNSBook/VPNGateway
ExpressRoute	https://aka.ms/AzNSBook/ExpressRoute
Virtual WAN	https://aka.ms/AzNSBook/VirtualWAN

Current threats and challenges

In July 2019, one of the largest data breaches ever was announced as Capital One was victim to an attack that led to more than 100 million account holders' information being stolen. The attacker had accessed Capital One's AWS (Amazon Web Services) instance through a miscon-figured WAF. The attacker tricked the firewall into relaying requests to a key back-end resource in the cloud. This resource is responsible for handing out temporary information including credentials. The WAF was assigned too many permissions, which allowed the attacker to list all files and read those files in any buckets. The attack was conducted by a single person who was ultimately arrested.

This example shows how connected network security and application security are. If you secure only one or the other, you leave your cloud infrastructure and applications vulnerable to attack. It's imperative that services deployed to the cloud are secured using a defense in-depth strategy. Figure 1-14 has a chart showing the number of accounts exposed in several data breaches.

Big-time breaches

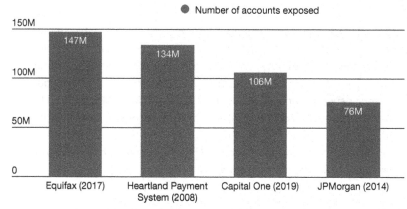

FIGURE 1-14 Chart of data breaches

Source: News reports

Data breaches continue to be on the rise as more companies shift to the cloud to expose end-user applications and services to their customers. There are a few ways these types of attacks occur but the attacks require that companies have holistic security programs to protect all aspects of their cloud deployment, starting with securing the network infrastructure the cloud applications use.

According to Verizon[1] and Trustwave[2] 2020 reports, cloud attacks have doubled and reached more than 20% of reported attacks. For the hacking vector, Verizon reported that web applications were at the top in 2020. As you can see in Figure 1-15, data is still the top cloud breach, and crypto mining continues even with its decline in 2018.

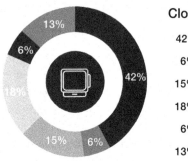

Cloud

42% Financial Data

6% CNP (E-commerce)

15% User Credentials

18% PII

6% Proprietary

13% Crypto Mining

FIGURE 1-15 Chart of cloud attack types from the Trustwave Global Security Report

Cloud computing creates new challenges for organizations because they can no longer control every aspect of the IT infrastructure and keep all assets behind their network perimeter. Organizations must adopt the cloud in some way to keep up with growing their business and customer needs. This means they will need to connect current on-prem networks to the cloud and create services in the cloud available to the global customer base. Ensuring seamless connection while creating secure networks becomes ever more complex. Azure provides native network security services to help customers achieve these.

One of the biggest challenges for organizations is implementing an appropriate security architecture. Chapter 2, "Secure Azure network architectures," covers creating a secure Azure network architecture. Most organizations run in a hybrid mode for some time, which requires running dual perimeters. In the classic perimeter model, network controls were enough. In the modern perimeter model, it moves to identity controls at many layers. Instead of just closing down a port or blocking an IP in the classic perimeter, modern perimeter requires that you contain attacks at all layers (network, application, identity, and data). This is also referred to as Zero Trust. This means administrators of IT and security must work together and that the security architecture is well-defined, understood, and adhered to by both sides. Figure 1-16 shows that attackers are using identity-based attacks, and organizations need to move from the classic network perimeter to an identity-based modern perimeter.

---

[1] You can read the Verizon 2020 Data Breach Investigations Report at https://aka.ms/AzNSBook/Verizon

[2] You can read the 2020 Trustwave Global Security Report at https://aka.ms/AzNSBook/Trustwave

NOTE To read more on Zero Trust, see *https://aka.ms/AzNSBook/ZeroTrust.*

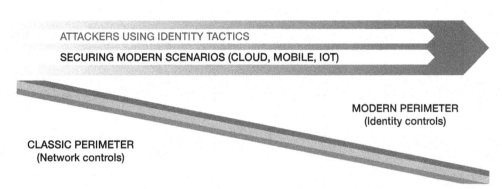

FIGURE 1-16 Dual perimeters

The base to any security architecture in the cloud is to understand the shared responsibility model. In all service types (SaaS, PaaS, IaaS), both Microsoft and the Customer have some responsibility. Customers frequently misunderstand where their responsibility is, which can lead to misconfiguration and from there to attacks. As the customer designs the security architecture, they need to account for their responsibility. For example, when deploying a multitier web application, the customer is no longer responsible for the operating system and thus doesn't need to run a host firewall but still needs to control network access to the application. For example, for an application that requires internal access, would ExpressRoute be enough to secure the app? This is not likely because an attacker could access the application from inside the customer network over the ExpressRoute.

Figure 1-17 shows the shared responsibility model in the cloud. It is important to understand this model. Organizations now share responsibility with the cloud provider. Moving higher in the stack means the cloud provider is more responsible than the organization.

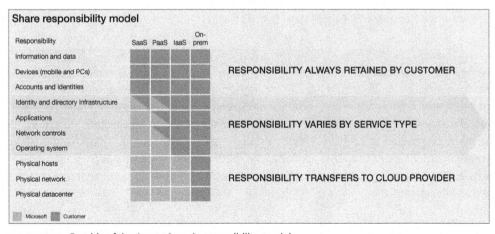

FIGURE 1-17 Graphic of the Azure shared responsibility model

Azure Network Security

Microsoft Azure runs in datacenters managed and operated by Microsoft. These are geo-graphically dispersed and comply with key industry standards, such as ISO/IEC 27001:2013 and NIST SP 800-53, for security and reliability. As a cloud provider, Microsoft must protect Azure to ensure a secure infrastructure customers can trust from hardening the datacenters and servers within them to ensuring access is controlled based on least privilege to monitoring and responding to attacks against the infrastructure. Figure 1-18 shows the various techniques and processes Microsoft uses to protect its cloud.

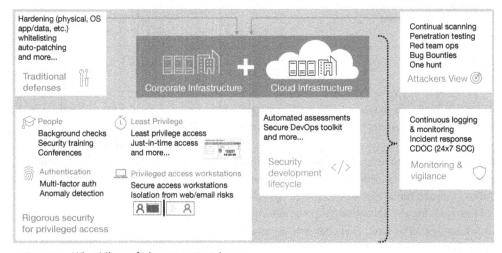

FIGURE 1-18   What Microsoft does to protect Azure

> **NOTE**   To read more on Azure Infrastructure Security,
> see *https://aka.ms/AzNSBook/AzSecurity.*

The Azure network architecture uses a modified version of the industry standard core/distribution/access model. Azure has two separate architectures. Some existing Azure custom-ers and shared services reside on the default LAN architecture (DLA), whereas new regions and virtual customers reside on Quantum 10 (Q10) architecture. The DLA architecture has active/passive access routers and security access control lists (ACLs) to them. The Q10 architecture is a mesh design where ACLs are not applied at the routers. Instead, ACLs are applied through software load balancing (SLB) or software-defined VLANs. Figure 1-19 is an overview of these two architectures.

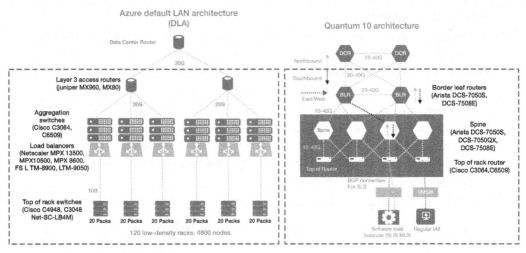

FIGURE 1-19 Azure Network Architectures

Filtering routers at the edge and access layer of the Azure network provides well-established security at the packet level. The routers help to ensure that the actual contents of the packets contain data in the expected format and conform to the expected client/server communication scheme. Azure implements a tiered architecture, consisting of the following network segregation and access control components:

- **Edge routers** These segregate the application environment from the internet. Edge routers are designed to provide anti-spoof protection and limit access by using ACLs.

- **Distribution (access) routers** These allow only Microsoft-approved IP addresses, provide anti-spoofing, and establish connections by using ACLs.

ACLs for virtual networks are implemented in Network Security Groups (NSGs). Chapter 2 covers NSGs and how you can layer them in with your network security architecture.

Distributed denial of service (DDoS) attacks continue to present a real threat to the reliability of online services. As attacks become more targeted and sophisticated, and as the services Microsoft provides become more geographically diverse, identifying and minimizing the effect of these attacks is a high priority. Microsoft provides DDoS Basic as part of the Azure platform for all customers. We discuss DDoS in depth in Chapter 6, "Mitigating DDoS attacks."

Core security and firewall features

Azure implements software security and firewall features at various levels to enforce security features that are usually expected in a traditional environment to protect the core security authorization boundary. These are different from Azure Firewall, which is covered in Chapter 3, "Controlling traffic with Azure Firewall." These firewalls protect the Azure service but still allow traffic to the customer environments.

Azure security features

Azure implements host-based software firewalls inside the production network. Several core security and firewall features reside within the core Azure environment. These security features reflect a defense-in-depth strategy within the Azure environment. Customer data in Azure is protected by the Hypervisor, native host, host, and guest firewalls.

Hypervisor firewall (packet filter) is implemented in the hypervisor and configured by the fabric controller (FC) agent. This firewall protects the tenant that runs inside the VM from unauthorized access. By default, when a VM is created, all traffic is blocked and then the FC agent adds rules and exceptions in the filter to allow authorized traffic.

Two categories of rules are programmed on hypervisor firewalls:

- **Machine config or infrastructure rules** By default, all communication is blocked. Exceptions exist that allow a VM to send and receive Dynamic Host Configuration Protocol (DHCP) communications and DNS information and send traffic to the "public" internet outbound to other VMs within the FC cluster and OS Activation server. Because the VMs' allowed list of outgoing destinations does not include Azure router subnets and other Microsoft properties, the rules act as a layer of defense for them.

- **Role configuration file rules** Defines the inbound ACLs based on the tenant's service model. For example, if a tenant has a web front end on port 80 on a certain VM, port 80 is opened to all IP addresses. If the VM has a worker role running, the worker role is opened only to the VM within the same tenant.

Azure Service Fabric and Azure Storage run on a native OS, which has no hypervisor and, therefore, Windows Firewall is configured with the preceding two sets of rules.

The host firewall protects the host partition, which runs the hypervisor. The rules are programmed to allow only the FC and jump boxes to talk to the host partition on a specific port. The other exceptions are to allow DHCP response and DNS replies. Azure uses a machine configuration file, which contains a template of firewall rules for the host partition. A host firewall exception also exists that allows VMs to communicate to host components, wire server, and metadata server, through specific protocol/ports.

The Windows Firewall piece of the guest OS is configurable by customers on customer VMs and storage.

An attacker on the internet cannot address traffic to those addresses because it would not reach Microsoft. Internet gateway routers filter packets that are addressed solely to internal addresses, so they would not enter the production network. The only components that accept traffic that's directed to VIPs are load balancers.

Firewalls that are implemented on all internal nodes have three primary security architecture considerations for any given scenario:

- Firewalls are placed behind the load balancer and accept packets from anywhere. These packets are intended to be externally exposed and would correspond to the open ports in a traditional perimeter firewall.

- Firewalls accept packets only from a limited set of addresses. This consideration is part of the defensive in-depth strategy against DDoS attacks. Such connections are cryptographically authenticated.
- Firewalls can be accessed only from select internal nodes. They accept packets only from an enumerated list of source IP addresses, all of which are dedicated IPs (DIPs) within the Azure network. For example, an attack on the corporate network could direct requests to these addresses, but the attacks would be blocked unless the source address of the packet was one in the enumerated list within the Azure network. The access router at the perimeter blocks outbound packets that are addressed to an address that's inside the Azure network because of its configured static routes.

Summary

In this chapter, we reviewed some of the core Azure networking concepts like the various services customers use. These are important to understand to enable application of Network Security services we will discuss throughout this book. We also covered how Microsoft protects its networks for its cloud. We covered some current threats and how they are applicable to network security. It's important to understand the threat and why network security is needed to protect cloud applications. Throughout this book, we will cover in depth each of the network security services Azure provides.

## Chapter 2

Secure Azure Network architectures

C hapter 1, "Introduction to Azure Network Security," covers some basics to Azure networks and the current threat landscape. Given this, it is ever more important to define your Azure network architecture to meet needs but allow for network security and containment in the event of a breach.

Many organizations used perimeter-based networks that assume all systems behind the perimeter are trusted. This type of network defense is obsolete. Zero Trust networks are the next evolution that eliminates the trust based on network location. Zero Trust typically integrates user and device information, such as location and health state, which is run through a policy engine to determine whether access should be permitted or denied. In Zero Trust, a user in the corporate office on a managed machine might be able to access a cloud-based highly sensitive application, but when they go home, the same access may be limited (block downloading) or denied.

Layering cloud security into your Azure deployments as part of a Zero Trust approach allows for limiting or containing an attack if it does occur. In a simple form, having all IaaS VMs on one subnet would allow an attacker to quickly pivot between machines. Breaking the machines into groups by function and moving them to separate virtual networks (vNet) and applying Network Security Groups (NSGs) to the virtual networks can prevent an attacker from pivoting at all.

This chapter explains the best practices to a good network architecture, various types of network architectures in Azure, and how network security services can be layered in to protect these architectures.

Best practices

Before diving into network architectures, it's important that we quickly mention Azure Well-Architected Framework. The framework consists of the following five pillars:

- Cost Optimization
- Operational Excellence
- Performance Efficiency

- Reliability
- Security

NOTE   To read more on Azure Well-Architected Framework, see
https://aka.ms/AzNSBook/AWAF.

The Azure Well-Architected Framework gives you a way to apply the best practices and principles to your applications or services. Security is one of the most important aspects of architecture. It provides assurance for the CIA (confidentiality, integrity, and availability) triad against attacks and loss of data. Losing these assurances can hurt an organization's reputation, business operations, and revenue. If you don't cost optimize your architecture, your return might be lower, but if you don't secure your architecture, there might be no returns at all.

Under the pillar of security, network security and containment is a key topic that organizations must adhere to for protecting their cloud deployments. Here are the best practices for network security and containment:

- Align network segmentation with enterprise segmentation strategy
- Centralize network management and security
- Evolve security beyond network controls
- Build a security containment strategy
    - Define an internet edge strategy
    - Decide on an internet ingress/egress policy
    - Mitigate DDoS attacks
    - Design virtual network security technology
- Decide use of legacy network security technology
- Enable enhanced network visibility

The first best practice is to align network segmentation with enterprise segmentation. Organizations need to define how they will segment the enterprise starting from the top so that all teams (identity, network, app teams, and so on) are building and working to the same strategy. The following graphic depicts a reference enterprise segmentation from the Well-Architected Framework. Here the organization has created a central identity store, uses Management Groups to apply central policies and permissions, and has broken networks into segments that align with enterprise segments of subscriptions and resources. Figure 2-1 shows a segmentation reference model that can be used as a starting point.

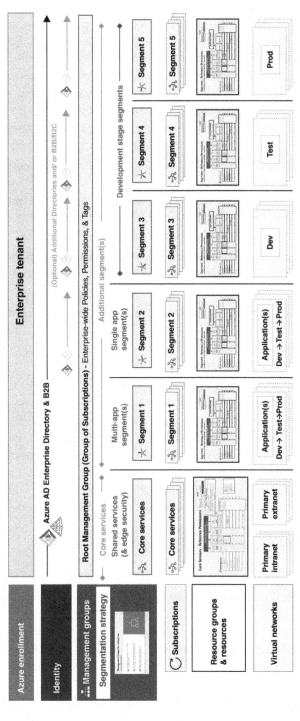

FIGURE 2-1 Reference model for segmentation

Under the core services, the organization has centralized network management and security. This is the second best practice for network security. By centralizing network management and security, the organization can prevent applications or segments from being created that do not adhere to the network security strategy. Very often organizations that don't centralize have new resources created in the cloud with a direct connection to the internet and little to no network security applied. This results in attacks against those resources that we know are unavoidable! Centralizing network management and security ensures new segments are protected and leverages the tools and expertise of the network and security teams. The following graphic depicts the reference for network security applied using the enterprise segmentation strategy. Figure 2-2 is a possible model for centralized network management and security.

In this design, the shared services segment is a hub virtual network providing core services, connectivity to on-prem, and public connectivity. By using this design, the organization can control ingress/egress (north-south) traffic from the hub and apply to all spokes. The next best practice is to define an internet edge strategy. Organizations need to choose how they will protect against from internet-based attacks. There are two primary choices:

- **Use cloud native controls, such as Azure Firewall and Web Application Firewall** This approach typically implements basic security that is good enough for common attacks but is well integrated into the platform.

- **Use partner virtual network appliances (available in the Azure Marketplace)** This approach often provides advanced features that protect against sophisticated attacks, but can cost more. An organization may also have existing knowledge/skills on the partner virtual network appliances.

The organization must decide based on experience and requirements. Once decided, the next detail is to apply ingress/egress policy baseline. In perimeter-based networks, many organizations would allow network traffic from internal to internet over HTTP/80 and HTTPS/443. This was fine until attackers started using HTTP(s) outbound to conduct command and control of exploited machines. In the era of Zero Trust, the concept starts with deny all outbound and only allows what is needed. It can't be as broad as HTTP(s), and it must be more restrictive to allow HTTP(s) to specific domain names. Using this approach makes it significantly harder for attackers because they can't use their command and control nodes and need to find another way.

Let's take a look at the ingress side, too. By using cloud native controls, instead of having to allow RDP/SSH inbound on the firewall, organizations can use services like Azure Bastion and Azure Security Center (ASC) Just-in-time VM (JIT) access. Azure Bastion allows remote management access using HTTPs and would not require opening the firewall at all. Because Bastion is integrated into the Azure portal, organizations could apply Azure Active Directory Conditional Access to the Azure portal, which would apply Zero Trust to remote management of VMs. ASC JIT integrates with Azure Firewall, which again means RDP/SSH would not need to be open all the time to all sources but could be opened on demand to only specific sources (client machine IP or a specific subnet). Both of these examples are part of the best practice to evolve security beyond network controls. They now factor in identity, device, and application as part of access to the VM incorporating Zero Trust principles.

Reference enterprise design - Azure network security

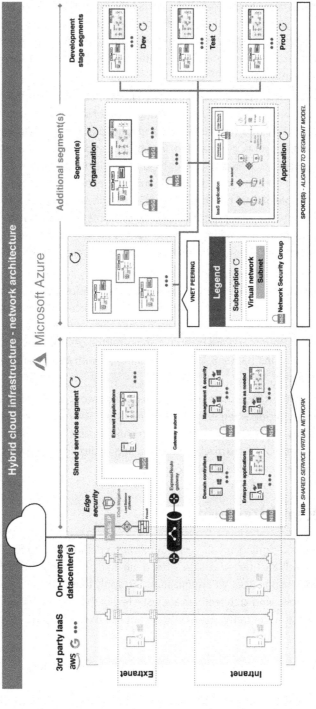

FIGURE 2-2 Centralized network management and security

For public-facing applications and services, it's imperative to protect against DDoS attacks. Cloud providers, including Azure, provide DDoS protection at the network layer to protect the platform. Organizations should also apply DDoS protection at higher layers to protect their applications. This type of protection typically profiles the application usage and uses machine learning to look for anomalous traffic. The service should proactively protect the application before degradation. Azure provides DDoS protection service, which is covered in Chapter 6, "Mitigating DDoS attacks."

Moving inward, organizations need to design network subnet security for their network segments. It is recommended that you plan for growth of resources in subnets over time and group resources in subnet by common roles and functions. Allow for larger IP address subnets on virtual networks to support expansion. If an organization has one subnet with five different resources, it needs to create NSG rules to support the different roles. Grouping resources allows for NSG configuration to be simplified and not get out of hand over time. It's important to apply the principle of least privilege at the NSG to limit and contain traffic between subnets and virtual networks (east-west traffic). If an attacker somehow makes it into a virtual machine, maybe due to an application vulnerability, they won't be able to pivot to other machines in other virtual networks. This is also referred to as micro-segmentation.

Organizations should enable enhanced network visibility as a best practice. Network logs should be integrated with the organization SIEM (security information and event management). This provides better visibility either through network log detection rules, the ability to query the data in the event of an incident for further investigation, or the ability to dashboard the data to look for trends and interesting changes for the central network and security teams. We cover monitoring in Chapter 8, "Security monitoring with Azure Sentinel, Security Center, and Network Watcher."

Lastly, organizations have some existing or legacy network security technologies, like IDS/IPS, that they must decide whether to bring to the cloud. The recommendation is to evaluate these technologies and favor newer Zero Trust technologies where appropriate and look to cloud-native versions of where machine learning and artificial intelligence can be provided to replace or advance these types of technologies.

Network architectures

When planning or designing any service or application deployment to the cloud it's imperative you start with a well-architected design. After defining a network strategy based on the previously discussed best practices, an organization can apply that to the architecture that meets their needs. The following architectures are just a few of the commonly used examples and how the best practices for network security are applied to them.

Cloud native

In recent years, it is entirely possible that a company was created and running with an entirely cloud-based set of services, which means they have no on-prem servers running, and they are using SaaS applications and hosting their service purely in the cloud. The following graphic depicts a simple cloud-native architecture where the organization might be using a few public services. The company has deployed its web application in Azure using purely PaaS services. This architecture is simple and can be secured by leveraging firewall features built into storage and SQL PaaS. Storage and SQL could be configured to block internet access and restrict it to the App Service web app. The following list covers some advantages and disadvantages:

- Advantages
  - Simple
  - Leverages network security services built into PaaS
- Disadvantages
  - Traffic is not routed through any central controlling service or device.
  - Each PaaS service has its own network security configuration.

Figure 2-3 shows a simple cloud-only set of services that an organization might be using.

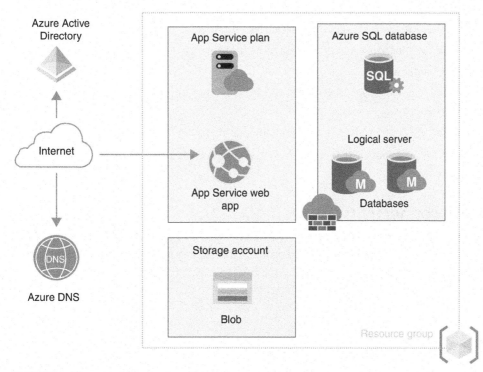

FIGURE 2-3 Diagram of cloud-only native services

As you can see from the next example, most architectures are not that simple. A startup may be, but as the company's service grows, it may need to expand to something more complex. Picture a company that has built a purely cloud-based application. It needs to deliver this application globally to its customers.

Here the application is global, which means traffic needs to be load balanced for both HTTP(s) and non-HTTP(s) traffic using Front Door and Traffic Manager. Front Door and Traffic Manager provide that load balancing. Web Application Firewall (WAF) is enabled on Front Door to defend the application at the network edge. Moving deeper in the stack, application gateway is then used in each region to load balance traffic to the VMs running the web application. WAF is also enabled on App Gateway to further protect the application. Why? WAF on Front Door supports geo-filtering, rate limiting, and Azure managed default rule sets, whereas WAF on App Gateway supports ModSec Core Rulesets (CRS). WAF is covered in depth in Chapter 5, "Secure application delivery with Azure Web Application Firewall." As another protection, DDoS Protection Standard is enabled in the tenant and applied to all virtual networks. DDoS protects any public IPs (PIP) of the application gateways in this architecture. DDoS is covered in Chapter 6. Lastly, NSGs are added to control east-west traffic. This layered approach provides additional defense in depth to the application. Following are the advantages and disadvantages:

- Advantages
    - Leverages network security at all layers.
    - Various network security services provide protection against many types of attacks.
- Disadvantages
    - Traffic between virtual networks is not routed through any central controlling service or device.
    - Each PaaS service has its own network security configuration.

Figure 2-4 is an architecture for a global web application with the various services used across the regions.

Hybrid connectivity

Next up are more common architectures used as there are many organizations with existing on-premise networks that need to be connected to Azure and their workloads deployed there.

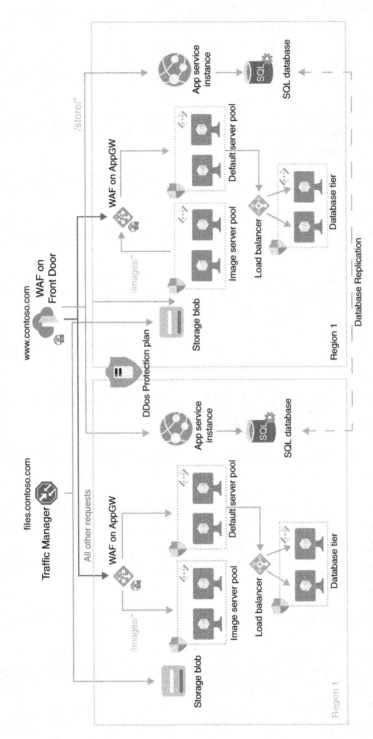

FIGURE 2-4 Complex global web application

ExpressRoute with VPN (ER/VPN) failover

In this architecture, ExpressRoute provides a connection that does not route over the internet and, in case of failure, a VPN backup path. The traffic is secured from on-premise to Azure. Once in Azure, WAF on App Gateway protects the web tier. Each subnet has an NSG to limit and contain traffic to only what is needed with rules appropriate for each subnet. For example, a rule to allow RDP or SSH from the management subnet IP range to the web tier and business tier IP range. The SQL database is configured with a service endpoint to provide direct connectivity to the service. No services or VMs have public internet access in this architecture. The following are the advantages and disadvantage:

- Advantages
  - Various network security provides protection against attacks.
  - Connectivity from on-premise is secure.
  - Remote management is secured from the management subnet only.
- Disadvantage
  - Traffic between virtual networks is not routed through any central controlling service or device.

Figure 2-5 is an ER/VPN architecture where on-premise connects to Azure over ExpressRoute and VPN.

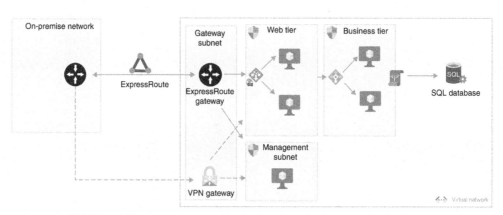

FIGURE 2-5 ER/VPN architecture

DMZ

The DMZ (demilitarized zone) architecture enables a secure hybrid network that extends an on-premises network to Azure. This forces traffic coming from on-premise bound for the internet to route through the network virtual appliance (NVA) in the cloud. The advantage to this design is that all traffic passes through the NVA, which can control and provide advanced inspection of the traffic. Because the NVA has a PIP, applying DDoS to protection against attacks adds another layer of protection to the workload. The following are the advantages and disadvantage:

- Advantages
  - Traffic is routed through a central device, which can control and limit traffic flows.
  - Various network security services provide protection against many types of attacks.
- Disadvantage
  - NVA requires additional management and configuration for HA.

Figure 2-6 shows the DMZ architecture and connections.

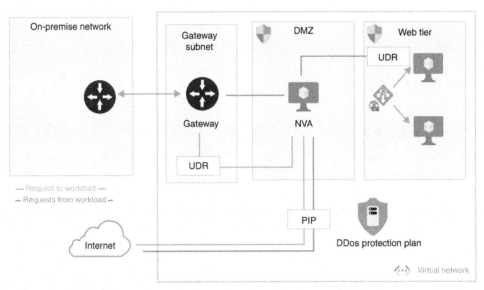

FIGURE 2-6 DMZ architecture

Expanding on this architecture, in Figure 2-7 we see that the architecture layers in Azure Bastion, which provides secure RDP (remote desktop protocol) and SSH (secure shell) access to the virtual machines. Azure Firewall has replaced the NVA to provide a cloud native approach. Azure Firewall has the advantages of being a fully managed PaaS. It can auto-scale as needed and provide built-in high availability. With an NVA, organizations must manage high availability, load balancing, and the appliance software themselves. Following are the advantages and disadvantage:

- Advantages
  - Cloud native services such as Azure Firewall and Bastion require less management and configuration.
  - Key traffic is routed through a central device, which can control and limit traffic flows.
  - Various network security services provide protection against many types of attacks.

- Disadvantage
  - Workloads are not fully isolated behind the firewall.

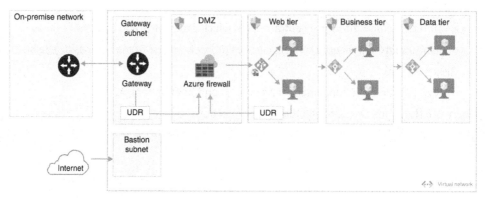

FIGURE 2-7 DMZ architecture with Azure Bastion

Hub and spoke

The hub virtual network acts as a central point of connectivity for on-premise networks, meaning on-prem is just another spoke. All traffic is routed through the hub virtual network. The spoke virtual networks create an isolated network to contain traffic to the specific workloads. This could be spokes for prod versus dev or workload or front end vs back end. Central services could be deployed in the hub as a separate subnet or a spoke virtual network. In the hub, Azure Firewall or an NVA is deployed to provide additional protection to east-west traffic between the spokes. This is an ideal architecture because it allows for expansion and contraction over time by adding or removing spokes. For multiregion, additional hubs are deployed to the region with region spokes connected. Hubs between regions can be connected using vNet peering, site-to-site VPN, or virtual WAN. The main difference between virtual WAN and hub and spoke is that virtual WAN is a managed offering. The following are the advantages and disadvantages:

- Advantages
  - Central services can provide cost savings by sharing them across workloads.
  - Hub virtual network can create separation of duties for IT (security, infrastructure) and workload (DevOps).
- Disadvantages
  - It is complex to manage as spoke numbers grow.
  - Spoke-to-spoke traffic must pass through the hub.

Figure 2-8 is a hub and spoke architecture.

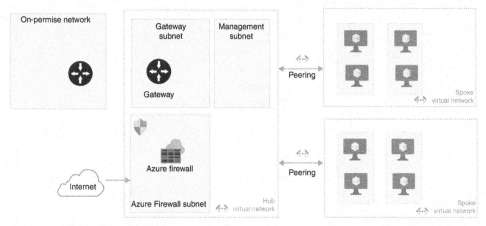

FIGURE 2-8 Hub-and-spoke architecture

Azure Virtual WAN

Azure vWAN is a service that brings together all of the benefits of previously discussed hybrid architectures into a single interface. Virtual WAN (vWAN) includes functionalities for branch, site-to-site VPN, point-to-site VPN, ExpressRoute, intra-cloud connectivity, routing, and Azure Firewall. vWAN is built on the hub and spoke architectures and enables global network connectivity.

The following resources are part of vWAN:

- **virtualWAN**   This resource is an overlay of the Azure network and contains multiple resources.

- **Hub**   This is a Microsoft-managed virtual network. It contains various endpoints like VPN Gateway and ExpressRoute gateway to provide connectivity to on-premise or mobile users.

- **Hub virtual network connections**   This is a connection resource to connect the hub to spoke virtual networks.

- **Hub-to-hub communication**   Hubs are deployed in regions and connected to each other in the virtual WAN. This creates a full-mesh architecture allowing traffic between virtual networks, on-premise, and branch sites.

- **Hub route table**   This allows the addition of routes to the hub route table.

Figure 2-9 is the basic diagram of vWAN.

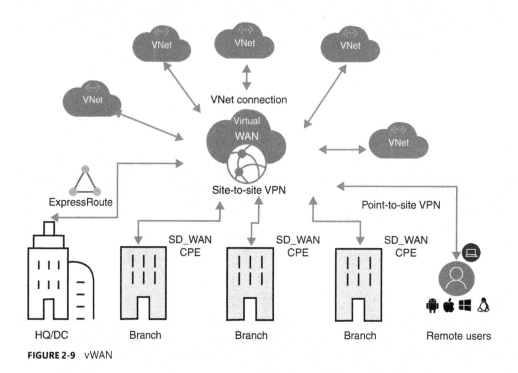

FIGURE 2-9 vWAN

Connectivity

Virtual WAN provides many types of connectivity, and the advantage is that an organization can use one or all of the various types. They can start with one that is needed today and expand over time as new connectivity requirements arise. There are various methods to connect on-premise to virtual WAN. Site-to-site VPN connections allow on-premise connectivity over an IPSec/IKE connection. Organizations must employ a VPN device or virtual WAN partner device on-premise to establish the S2S VPN. If there is a need for mobile users to have VPN access, a virtual WAN can be configured to provide VPN for users and require a VPN client on the endpoint. ExpressRoute lets organizations connect over a private connection.

Transit connectivity is also provided in virtual WAN. Once connected to the hub, on-premise traffic can be routed to spoke virtual networks. This means user traffic coming from on-prem will route over S2S VPN or ExpressRoute, hit the hub, and use the virtual network connection to the spoke to reach a server. This traverses the same path the opposite way. Virtual WAN also allows transit connectivity between VPN and ExpressRoute. A mobile user over VPN could reach on-premise via the hub. Spoke virtual networks can talk to each other through the hub.

Traffic can travel between two spokes via the hub. Multiple hubs can be added to virtual WAN as well. This will allow spoke virtual networks to talk over the hub-to-hub connection going from spoke to hub to the other hub to the other spoke.

Security

Virtual WAN allows organizations to apply virtual hub routing and manage traffic flow within the virtual WAN. Specifically, this can be used to isolate virtual networks, create shared services virtual networks, or route traffic through one of the Azure partner NVAs or Azure Firewall. There is also an option to use Azure Firewall in the hub and integrate partner offerings like zScaler, iBoss, and Checkpoint. In this configuration, Azure Firewall protects private traffic in the hubs and internet/SaaS traffic is routed to the partner service. An organization might have a need to isolate the virtual networks allowing traffic from on-premise to all virtual networks but not virtual network to virtual network. Or perhaps, the organization wants to configure shared services such as domain controllers or file services but doesn't want to allow all virtual network to virtual network traffic. By applying routing these scenarios are achievable.

> **NOTE**   To route traffic in a virtual WAN, it must be a standard type virtual WAN. See more at *aka.ms/AzNSBook/vWAN*.

In the Shared Services example, nonshared services virtual networks do not learn routes to other nonshared virtual networks but do learn about the shared services virtual network. Shared services are propagated to all virtual networks and branches/VPN using the default table. It is important to understand how routing can be used to limit traffic to only sources and destinations needed. Figure 2-10 depicts an example of the shared services routing.

To layer in security, organizations can deploy an NVA into a virtual network. When using NVA, spokes must be created off of the NVA virtual network that resides in the virtual WAN. This will allow having traffic from workload virtual networks to pass through the NVA. Figure 2-11 shows the NVA VNet added with spokes behind it.

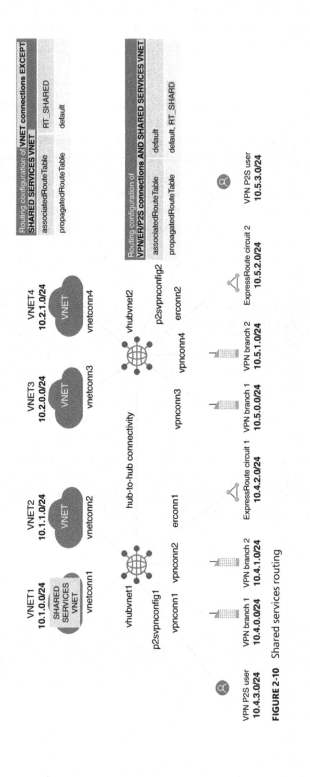

FIGURE 2-10 Shared services routing

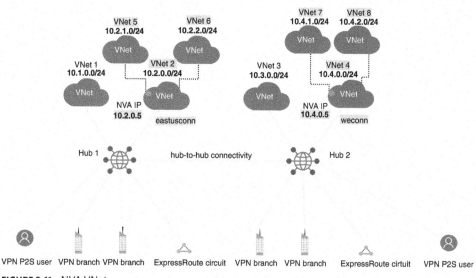

FIGURE 2-11 NVA VNet

If an organization wants to use cloud native network security, vWAN offers a secure virtual hub, which includes an Azure Firewall instead of using an NVA. Figure 2-12 shows the difference that additional spoke networks are not needed because Azure Firewall can be deployed in the vWAN hub.

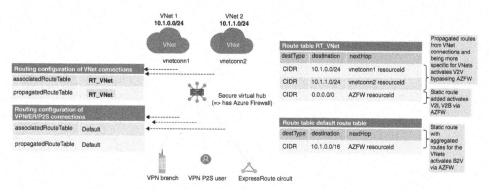

FIGURE 2-12 vWAN with Azure Firewall

Summary

In this chapter, we covered the importance of using Azure Well-Architected Framework to use best practices when designing networks and network security in Azure. We then reviewed various network architectures that can be used to deploy services and applications in Azure. Each architecture has its advantages and disadvantages and allows for network security in different ways. It is important to leverage the framework at the start and use those practices combined with the sample architectures to meet the needs and requirements of the application being deployed.

## Chapter 3

Controlling traffic with Azure Firewall

Azure Firewall is a platform-as-a-service (PaaS) stateful firewall. The PaaS aspect of Azure Firewall is a unique feature among firewalls. To understand what Azure Firewall is, it can be helpful to first understand what it is not. It is not the same thing as, nor does it replace, Network Security Groups (NSGs). Azure Firewall is not the same as the per-resource PaaS firewalls found on services such as Azure Key Vault. Rather, Azure Firewall is a PaaS service meant to exist in a virtual network (VNet) for the purpose of centrally controlling traffic. Firewall has a growing set of capabilities to detect threats, but the focus of this chapter will be on network segmentation.

Why Azure Firewall Exists

As customers move to the cloud, redesigning their digital workloads, network security is top of mind and a key enabler. Most enterprise customers require some application-level outbound traffic filtering to enable secure access to various internet resources. Additionally, customers need to segment and log access between cloud workloads and in hybrid connections. We found that customers are struggling with adopting their traditional Next Generation Firewall solutions in the cloud. Instead, they were looking for cloud-native, autoscalable, and highly available solutions to support their journey.

Azure Firewall was our response to that need. It is a cloud-native firewall-as-a-service offering that enables customers to centrally govern and log all their traffic flows using a DevOps approach. The service supports both application- and network-level filtering rules and is integrated with the Microsoft Threat Intelligence feed for filtering known malicious IP addresses and domains. Azure Firewall is highly available with built-in autoscaling.

Azure Firewall Manager was launched to address the rapid adoption of Azure Firewall. It is a cloud-native, central security management service for cloud-based security perimeters. It simplifies configuration, route management, and deployment for Azure Firewall today and will be extended to support additional network security services in the future.

Yair Tor, Principal PM manager

The role of Azure Firewall in secure architecture

While there are likely as many working Azure network architectures as there are Azure customers, the best practice we focus on is the hub-and-spoke design. Examples given can be applied to other architectures.

Network segmentation for security

Segmenting networks has long been a practice of secure architecture, and it makes sense to continue the practice in Azure networks. The days of perimeter-only defenses are a thing of the distant past, and one of the simplest and most effective ways to design a secure network is to apply segmentation.

Network segmentation, at a very basic level, amounts to applying the principle of least privilege to network traffic. This principle is most often applied to identities in the form of user authorization, but it holds up equally well when applied elsewhere, such as network access. Applied this way, security professionals can work toward the goal of allowing sources of network traffic (usually IP addresses) to access only the network destinations that are required for the source to perform its specific function.

Configuring networks with least privilege as the goal has several benefits for security. Applied to internal or (PaaS), traffic, least privilege can slow or prevent lateral movement within a network by an attacker or malicious insider. Applied to inbound traffic, limiting access to resources can significantly reduce the attack surface. Finally, using a strict positive security model, in which you allow only what is needed versus denying only what is known to be malicious, is a best practice that should be followed whenever possible. Especially in server environments, there is very rarely any need to allow outbound traffic more broadly than a few required destinations. Attackers and their tools have clever methods of exfiltrating data and communicating with command and control infrastructure, but without limiting outbound network access, even the least-clever attacker can be allowed to succeed.

Network segmentation and least privilege access are hardly the most exciting tools in the security practitioner's arsenal, but the fact is that they work. Of course, one would not argue that these are the only steps needed to secure an Azure network, but good network segmentation can be an excellent foundation for a more comprehensive defense in depth strategy.

What is Azure Firewall?

Azure Firewall is a managed service that is highly available, is autoscaling, and serves the purpose of securing Azure networks centrally by directing and inspecting traffic.

Although it is tempting to think of "an Azure Firewall" or "the Azure Firewall," it is more accurate to think of Azure Firewall as the service that it is. Rather than being a singular device, Azure Firewall exists as collection of resources managed by Azure. These underlying resources include load balancing and compute, but none of this needs to be managed by customers.

Even though the internal workings of the Azure Firewall instance are not exposed to users, the service still lives within a VNet alongside all the other resources on the network. In this way, Azure Firewall provides all the benefits of a PaaS service while being closely integrated with the Infrastructure as a Service (IaaS) and other resources that can exist on a typical VNet.

Understanding Firewall components

Azure Firewall has a few main components that can best be understood by viewing the requirements of a typical resource deployment. When you use the Azure portal to create a new Firewall, the requirements and main components can be seen in the **Basics** tab as pictured in Figure 3-1.

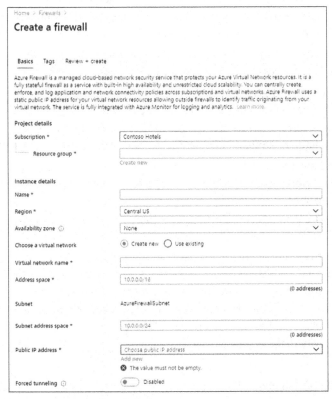

FIGURE 3-1 Azure Firewall deployment options

- **Subscription** An existing Azure Subscription must be selected. Note that Azure Firewall can accept traffic from any device that can route to it, regardless of Subscription.

- **Resource Group** A new or existing Resource Group can be used.

- **Name** The name of the Firewall must be unique within the Resource Group.

- **Region** Azure Firewall is available in all commercial regions, as well as most Government regions.

- **Availability Zone** One or more may be selected for increased availability and redundancy. Using Availability Zones guarantees a higher service-level agreement (SLA) because it gives Azure Firewall the ability to survive a datacenter failure.

- **Choose A Virtual Network** In the hub-and-spoke architecture example, Azure Firewall is deployed in the existing hub VNet. For best performance, this hub should be in the same region as the spokes, and the architecture should be duplicated in all required regions. To use an existing VNet to deploy a new Azure Firewall, a subnet named AzureFirewallSubnet must already exist.

- **Subnet** Azure Firewall must always be deployed to a subnet named AzureFirewallSubnet. This subnet is created automatically if a new VNet is being used to deploy Azure Firewall. This subnet must already exist if using an existing VNet to create a new Azure Firewall. This subnet can be as small as a /26 subnet. Once created, this subnet is reserved only for Azure Firewall and cannot be used by any other resources.

- **Public IP Address** A new or existing standard SKU public IP address is required for any Azure Firewall. More IP addresses can be added if required for NAT scenarios.

- **Forced Tunneling** By default, all traffic from Azure Firewall is routed to the internet, but traffic can be routed to another destination using forced tunneling if required. This configuration can only be done when creating a new Azure Firewall. We discuss forced tunneling in greater depth later in the chapter in the "Forced tunneling" section.

The most important concepts here are the VNet and subnet configurations because they must fit within the overall Azure network architecture that is being used. It is important to understand that the AzureFirewallSubnet is one that fits within the IP space of the VNet it exists in, but it's also not fully controlled by the customer. The reason for this is that the back-end components that comprise this PaaS service exist within this subnet and are managed by Microsoft.

Another important concept is the requirement for a Public IP Address. Because Azure Firewall is a PaaS service that exists within a private network, the public IP address must exist even if no customer traffic is being passed inbound or outbound (that is, if Azure Firewall is only controlling internal traffic). Microsoft needs the ability to communicate with the Azure Firewall to manage configuration, so a public IP address is a requirement. This does not, however, enable any other type of connectivity to the resource.

Getting traffic to Azure Firewall

Azure Firewall can control only the traffic that is routed to it, so aside from deploying the resource in a subnet, there are other steps that must be taken to integrate the service into the overall architecture.

Virtual network peering

In a hub-and-spoke architecture, the hub and each spoke are separate VNets. Each VNet is by default an isolated IP address space, meaning that traffic cannot pass from one VNet to another. The hub-and-spoke architecture takes advantage of the security of this inbuilt network segmentation by only extending connectivity between VNets when it is necessary. Peering is used to enable connectivity between VNets, specifically between the hub and each spoke. Spokes are not peered to each other.

Peering is configured on each VNet that requires connectivity to another. To enable bidirectional connectivity, peering must be configured on both VNets. The concepts involved in VNet peering are shown in Figure 3-2.

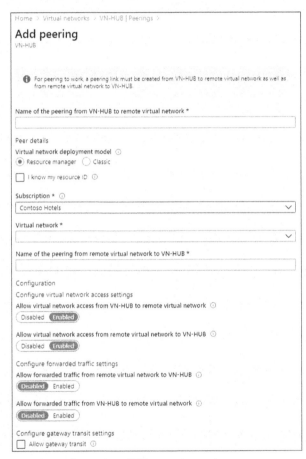

FIGURE 3-2 Screenshot of VNet peering options

- **Name Of The Peering From [Your VNet] To Remote Virtual Network** A unique name for the peering configuration. Each direction of the peering configuration will have a separate, unique name.

- **Virtual Network Deployment Model**   Resource manager is the default and most common option. Choose the option that applies to both VNets being peered.
- **Subscription**   This is the subscription of the remote network.
- **Virtual Network**   The remote virtual network.
- **Name Of The Peering From Remote Virtual Network To [Your VNet]**   A unique name for the peering configuration. Each direction of the peering configuration has a separate, unique name.
- **VNet Access**   These settings allow communication between resources in either network and extend the Virtual Network Service Tag to both peered networks.
- **Forwarded Traffic**   These settings allow traffic forwarded from other networks to traverse the peering.
- **Gateway Transit**   This setting allows traffic from a peered network to use a VPN Gateway. This is useful in configurations where the hub VNet is connected to an on-premise network via VPN.

Routing

Route tables are used to send traffic from any peered network to Azure Firewall. Route tables are assigned to subnets and contain one or many individual routes. These routes specify the next hop for traffic originating from given ranges.

There are several default routes that are put in place upon creation of VNets and subnets, peering configurations, and service endpoints. Routes created by Azure users are known as user defined routes, or UDRs. UDRs take precedence over Default routes, so can be used to direct traffic to destinations other than what is specified by default.

To route traffic from a subnet to Azure Firewall, a route table must be applied to that subnet to direct the traffic. The components of a user defined route table are shown in Figure 3-3.

FIGURE 3-3   Route settings

- **Address Prefix**   The destination range the route applies to. This is specified in CIDR notation, and any traffic bound for the specified range is subject to this route. In the example, 0.0.0.0/0 means that the route will be applied to all traffic.

- **Next Hop Type** The choices for this option are Virtual Network Gateway, Virtual Network, Internet, Virtual Appliance, or None. Azure Firewall falls into the category of virtual appliance for this purpose.

- **Next Hop Address** Specifies the IP address of the next hop destination. In this case it is the private IP address of Azure Firewall.

A route table can contain several routes, all applying to different portions of traffic, but in the example being used, all traffic is covered by a single route. Once a route has been added to a table, the route table must be applied to subnets, as shown in Figure 3-4.

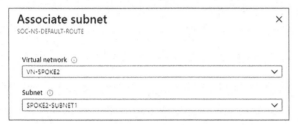

FIGURE 3-4 Route table to subnet association

Once applied to the necessary subnets, the new routes exist alongside the default routes. To observe the full route table applied to a given interface on a VNet, effective routes can be viewed as an option in the route table resource. This view is shown in Figure 3-5.

FIGURE 3-5 Effective routes

Note that there are two routes applied to the destination 0.0.0.0/0: one default route and one UDR. Because both apply to the same traffic and UDRs take precedence, the default route is changed to an invalid state. Azure prioritizes routes in the order of user defined, BGP, and default system routes. Although system routes cannot be changed or deleted, they can be overridden using UDRs or BGP routes.

Once routes have been applied to the applicable subnets, traffic matching the address prefixes (in this case, all traffic) is routed to Azure Firewall for processing.

Integrating with other traffic management

Azure Firewall is often not the only tool used to manage traffic on a network, and there are various ways to integrate with other tools, both Azure native and third party. It is helpful to think about the roles each service plays and plan to use the right tools for each job with minimal overlap and minimal conflict.

Network Security Groups

Network security groups, or NSGs, are a fundamental network control that are applied to network interfaces or subnets to apply access control rules to network traffic. The basic function is similar to that of Azure Firewall, so decisions need to be made on how best to apply each.

There are several differences between NSGs and Azure Firewall, but the biggest is the fact that NSGs are decentralized, whereas Azure Firewall is centrally managed. In many scenarios, it is wise to centralize traffic management rather than having to manage many NSGs at scale.

Even when using Azure Firewall, it is still common to use NSGs in addition to Firewall. The peering arrangement discussed previously in this chapter enables connectivity between hub-and-spoke VNets, and Azure Firewall restricts this flow of traffic to only allowed sources and destinations. However, any traffic not routed to Azure Firewall needs to be controlled by NSGs. To help determine the best architecture using some combination of Azure Firewall and NSGs, consider the following scenarios:

- **Azure Firewall only**   For this option, routes would be set up to force traffic through the Firewall for subnet-to-subnet traffic within the same VNet. This option provides segmentation and central control of traffic but increases the complexity of traffic flow. Although it is somewhat less efficient to send traffic to the Firewall in the peered hub, the fact that subnets can be isolated without the use of NSGs can be advantageous in terms of management overhead.

- **Azure Firewall with subnet NSGs**   In this example, routes would be set up to forward traffic to the Firewall only when it is bound outside the VNet. Subnet-to-subnet traffic is routed directly, without hitting Azure Firewall. Because it is most common for the boundary of trust to be at the subnet level, NSGs would need to be put in place on the subnets to control traffic flow between them.

Ultimately, the design depends on a number of factors, including internal security policy, risk tolerance, and management complexity. More architectural options are discussed in Chapter 9, "Combining Azure resources for a wholistic network security strategy."

Azure Private Link

Azure Private Link is a service that allows mapping of PaaS services to private IP addresses within VNets. This capability enables control and segmentation of traffic bound to supported PaaS services using Azure Firewall. The IP addresses of Azure private endpoints, which is the component of Private Link that exists on a VNet, can be used as the destination of Azure Firewall Network Rules.

Ideally private endpoints would live in a spoke VNet, and network access would be managed by Azure Firewall the same way access to any other VNet service would be controlled.

You also can use Private Link to integrate services owned and maintained by a managed service provider into the VNet of the consumer of the service. In this manner, even services managed by external providers can be subject to granular network access controls. Refer to Figure 3-6 for a diagram of Private Link components.

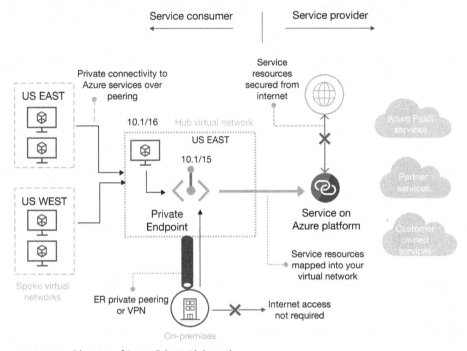

FIGURE 3-6 Diagram of Azure Private Link service

Network virtual appliances

Before Azure Firewall, network virtual appliances (NVAs) were the only way to centrally manage and secure network traffic in Azure. Now that another option exists, the two options could seem mutually exclusive. However, there are ways for both to be deployed either alongside one another or in parallel.

Azure Firewall and an NVA, or more accurately a load balanced set of NVAs, perform a very similar function. There are advantages to either option. Azure Firewall has the following potential advantages:

- Native to Azure, so integrated with many other components
- Managed using Azure Portal, PowerShell, CLI, API, or ARM
- Autoscaling to handle increased load

NVAs have the following potential advantages:

- Cloud platform independent
- Familiar set of features that have likely been used in on-premise networks before workloads migrated to Azure

Ultimately, the best tool for the job should be chosen, which does not mean that either an NVA or Azure Firewall has to be the only tool for every job. In many situations, the long-term strategy is to migrate to platform-native tools, but not every workload is suited to an immediate migration. For companies that have been using Azure for a long time, network appliances have likely been part of the architecture since the beginning, and migrating will best be done gradually. If a company is new to Azure or deploying a new workload to a greenfield environment, it is easier to integrate Azure Firewall into the plan.

The following scenarios are possible when using both Azure Firewall and NVAs to control traffic:

- **Isolated**   In this scenario, Azure Firewall would be deployed in hub VNets where appropriate, and NVAs would not exist at all in the hub or the peered VNets. The opposite would be true in networks where NVAs are deployed. Each would be selected to be the sole firewall in the network space where they are deployed. This architecture is the most common and least complex.

- **Side-by-side**   Complexity is higher in this example because Azure Firewall and an NVA would be deployed in the same network space, likely both in the same hub. Using routes, traffic from some VNets and subnets would be routed to Azure Firewall, and some routed to the NVA based on requirements. This scenario assumes that resources sharing subnets or VNets also share the same networking requirements.

- **In-line**   This architecture makes use of forced tunneling (described later in the chapter) to send traffic from Azure Firewall to an NVA before leaving the network. All traffic from peered VNets would route to the Azure Firewall, but rather than egressing directly to the internet, traffic is passed to another device. This is useful when Azure Firewall is the best tool for east-west traffic, but there are requirements for specific or central inspection for egress traffic.

These architectures and others will be discussed in greater depth in Chapter 9.

Advanced features

Aside from basic traffic control using the various rule types available (discussed in a later section), Azure Firewall has several settings that need to be configured as part of the deployment process.

Managing DNS requests, both from Firewall and from the clients on the networks it protects, can be done in different ways. Using the DNS proxy and custom DNS settings, along with the virtual network DNS settings, administrators can control how DNS traffic is managed.

Outbound traffic leaving Azure Firewall can either go straight to the internet or be routed to another device. Forced tunneling allows for the option of using other appliances to perform additional inspection on outbound traffic.

Azure Firewall now offers several features for traffic inspection and threat detection. These features, including threat intelligence, IDS/IPS, and TLS termination, are discussed briefly in this chapter and more thoroughly in Chapter 4, "Traffic inspection in Azure networks."

DNS settings

By default, Azure Firewall uses Azure DNS for all name resolution. In most cases, this works fine, but there are options available if name resolution needs to be handled by a different internal or external service.

There are two options to consider when setting up Azure Firewall for custom DNS: DNS servers and DNS proxy. You can find these settings on the DNS blade of either Azure Firewall or Azure Firewall Manager Policy. Figure 3-7 shows DNS settings in an Azure Firewall Policy.

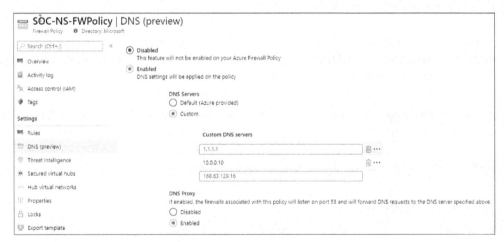

FIGURE 3-7 Azure Firewall DNS settings

- **DNS server** These are the destination servers that Azure Firewall will send DNS requests to. Requests can either be from Azure Firewall itself, in the case of resolving FQDNs on behalf of clients to forward outbound traffic, or they could be query traffic proxied from clients on the network.

- **DNS proxy**   This option configures Azure Firewall to listen on port 53 for requests, which it then forwards to the configured DNS servers. It is recommended that you enable this when using custom DNS so that clients and Azure Firewall resolve names the same way.

If using DNS proxy, DNS servers on any VNets routing traffic to Azure Firewall can simply be set to the IP address of the Firewall. Virtual network DNS settings are shown in Figure 3-8.

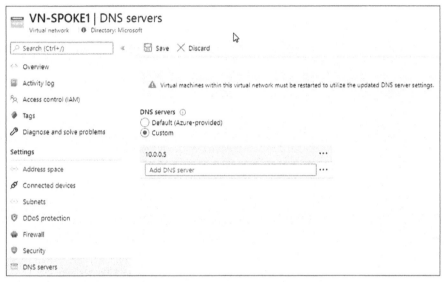

FIGURE 3-8   Virtual network DNS settings

The ability to configure DNS behavior on Azure Firewall is especially useful in scenarios where internal FQDNs are used for service communication within a network. When Azure Firewall is configured to use the same DNS that clients use, FQDNs can be used in Network rules (discussed later in the chapter), which tend to be much easier to manage than IP addresses.

Another advantage of enabling DNS proxy on Azure Firewall is that all DNS traffic will be processed by the Firewall. This is advantageous not only because Firewall rules will be applied to the traffic, but because security mechanisms such as threat intelligence and IDS/IPS will be applied to the traffic, and everything will be logged centrally.

Forced tunneling

By default, Azure Firewall is the last hop for traffic bound for the internet. If Azure Firewall receives outbound traffic, it gets forwarded directly to the internet. Forced tunneling provides the option to change this behavior and set another destination as the hop after Azure Firewall. This can be useful in architectures where it is required to send all traffic to some central inspection service or hairpin traffic back to on-premise hardware.

Forced tunneling can only be configured when an Azure Firewall is first deployed. If the Forced Tunneling option is set to Enabled during deployment, there are some extra configuration options that need to be set, as shown in Figure 3-9.

FIGURE 3-9 Azure Firewall forced tunneling settings

The major change to take into account when deploying Azure Firewall in forced tunneling mode is that another subnet is created and a public IP address is assigned for management use. The reason for these additions is to ensure that Azure can still manage the Firewall even when outbound traffic is routed to another destination.

It is important to note that the actual routing of traffic to the required destination is not done on the Azure Firewall but rather by adding routes to the AzureFirewallSubnet that is created with Firewall. Without the Forced Tunneling option enabled and the management subnet configured, adding routes to AzureFirewallSubnet would not be permitted and would break the operation of the service.

SNAT Control

In the default configuration, Azure Firewall performs Source Network Address Translation (SNAT) on all traffic bound for any public destination, meaning that the source of the packet is changed to the public IP of the Firewall. This is standard behavior of edge devices, but there are scenarios where preserving the original source is desirable.

In the case of forced tunneling, if outbound traffic is forwarded to another appliance from Azure Firewall, that traffic is SNAT'd by Firewall, and the original source is unknown to the appliance. In this case, it is best to disable SNAT for the IP of the downstream appliance to preserve the original source.

Another scenario when SNAT would not be needed is if public IP ranges are used inside a private network alongside IANA RFC 1918 addresses. Although this may not be the most common scenario, it can be addressed by configuring Firewall not to SNAT for those destinations.

Configuration of private IP ranges (the destination ranges that Azure Firewall will not SNAT to) can be configured on the **Overview** blade of the Firewall, as shown in Figure 3-10.

Also note that if required, Firewall can be configured to SNAT all traffic by entering 255.255.255.255/32 as the range or never to SNAT by entering 0.0.0.0/0.

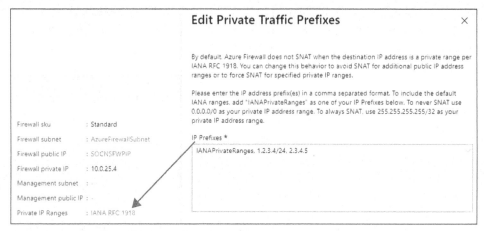

FIGURE 3-10 Azure Firewall SNAT configuration (private IP ranges)

Traffic inspection

This chapter focuses on using Azure Firewall to control traffic flow for security and connectivity, but it makes sense to briefly mention the inspection capabilities of Azure Firewall before covering them more thoroughly in Chapter 4 (along with inspection capabilities of other services).

Like any other network security appliance or service, Azure Firewall has capabilities to do more than just direct traffic that is forwarded to it. It can also apply various types of inspection to the traffic for security.

- **Threat intelligence** Integrated with Microsoft's internal threat feeds, Azure Firewall can block inbound traffic from known malicious IP addresses or outbound traffic to malicious FQDNs or IP addresses.

- **TLS termination** Azure Firewall can terminate outbound traffic to decrypt and analyze the full packets. This capability enables other inspection types, both those that are currently existing and planned for the future.

- **IDS/IPS** Signature-based intrusion detection and prevention can be applied to traffic for the purpose of blocking malicious traffic. While IDS/IPS can be applied to encrypted or clear-text traffic, decrypting traffic naturally enables more complete inspection.

- **Full URL filtering** The ability to decrypt traffic has the added benefit of being able to see the full URL rather than just the host that is readable from encrypted packets. Using the full URL in rules allows security teams to be more specific in what traffic is allowed and blocked and enriches log data generated by Azure Firewall.

This set of inspection capabilities is shorter than what some NVAs can provide, but this is continually being updated. Azure Firewall has only been generally available since 2018 and will continue to grow in capability and maturity as time passes.

Rule types

When Azure Firewall is first deployed into the hub VNet and traffic starts to be routed to it, the default behavior is to block all traffic. It is possible to override this behavior by creating a rule that allows all traffic, but this is not advisable from a security perspective in nearly all cases. Rather, a positive security model should be followed to allow traffic only when the function of the systems involved directly requires it.

There are three different rule types that can be configured to allow traffic through Azure Firewall, including Network Rules, Application Rules, and DNAT Rules. These rules are organized into groups and can be created and managed either directly on individual Firewall instances via the Rules blade or using Firewall Policies with Firewall Manager.

Network rules

Network rules are used to control traffic within the private network space or east-west traffic. To understand the components and options available, create a new rule collection on a Firewall from the portal as shown in Figure 3-11.

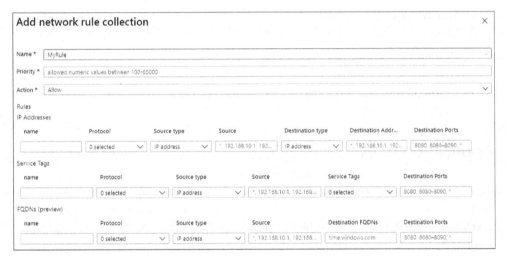

FIGURE 3-11 Azure Firewall network rules

Network rule collections have the following general options:

- **Name**   This is a unique name for the collection, which can be up to 80 characters long and can be used to include relevant information used for rule auditing over time.
- **Priority**   Number from 100 to 65,000 that specifies in which order the collection is processed. Lower numbers are processed first. It is advised that you space out rule collection priority so new collections can be inserted between existing ones as needed.
- **Action**   This is the result when traffic matches a rule: Allow or Deny.

A network rule collection can have multiple individual rules associated, which inherit settings from the collection, such as Priority and Action. The rules are grouped by the destination type, which can be IP Address, Service Tags, or FQDNs. The options for individual rules include:

- **Name**   This is a unique name within the rule.

- **Protocol**   The protocol can be set to TCP, UDP, ICMP, or Any. Multiselect is also allowed.

- **Source Type**   The source type can be either IP Address or IP Group. IP Groups are extremely useful in this context because they can be managed separately from the rules that use them, enabling IP Groups to be dynamic without having to constantly change Firewall configuration.

- **Source**   Sources can be a comma-separated list of IP addresses and CIDR blocks, *, or a multiselect list of IP Groups, if that is the type.

- **Destination Type**   This is only available for IP address rules and can be either IP Address or IP Group.

- **Destination Address**   Destinations can be a comma-separated list of IP addresses and CIDR blocks, *, or a multiselect list of IP Groups, if that is the type.

- **Service Tags**   This is a multiselect list of available Service Tags, which correspond to Microsoft-managed lists of IP addresses and ranges associated with common services.

- **Destination FQDNs**   This is a comma-separated list of FQDNs and requires DNS Proxy to be enabled to ensure that resolution is the same for clients and Azure Firewall.

- **Destination Ports**   Ports can be specified in a comma-separated list of individual ports, ranges, or *.

Application rules

Application rules control outbound traffic from the network to the internet. In server environments, internet access should be restricted to only what is essential, and Application Rules can be used to manage a list of allowed destinations. Create an application rule collection by selecting **Add Application Rule** from the **Application Rule tab** of the **Rules** blade as shown in Figure 3-12.

The options available for the collection are

- **Name**   This is a unique name for the collection—up to 80 characters long—which can be used to include relevant information used for rule auditing over time.

- **Priority**   Number from 100 to 65,000 that specifies in which order the collection is processed. Lower numbers are processed first. It is advised that you space out rule collection priority so new collections can be inserted between existing ones as needed.

- **Action**   This is the result when traffic matches a rule: Allow or Deny.

FIGURE 3-12 Azure Firewall DNS settings

Individual rules are grouped by the destination type, either FQDN tags or target FQDNs, and have the following options:

- **Name**   This is a unique name within the rule.
- **Source Type**   The source type can be either IP Address or IP Group. IP Groups are extremely useful in this context because they can be managed separately from the rules that use them, enabling IP Groups to be dynamic without having to constantly change Firewall configuration.
- **Source**   Sources can be a comma-separated list of IP addresses and CIDR blocks, *, or a multiselect list of IP Groups, if that is the type.
- **Protocol:Port**   Protocol and optional port can be specified here in a comma-separated list of protocols (HTTP, HTTPS, or MSSQL). If a nonstandard port is used, it can be specified after the protocol—for example, HTTP:8080.
- **FQDN Tags**   Supported FQDN Tags include MicrosoftActiveProtectionService, WindowsDiagnostics, WindowsUpdate, AppServiceEnvironment, AzureBackup, AzureKubernetesService, HdInsight, and WindowsVirtualDesktop.
- **Target FQDNs**   These are represented in a comma-separated list, which can include wildcards such as *.microsoft.com.

DNAT rules

Destination network address translation (DNAT) rules can be used to allow traffic into the network from the internet. DNAT rules forward specified external traffic to internal destinations, which is useful for centrally managing access to internal resources without having to assign public IP addresses to each service. This is commonly used for allowing management access to servers or to make an internal web application available outside the network. You create a DNAT rule collection in the same way that you create application or network rule collections. This is shown in Figure 3-13.

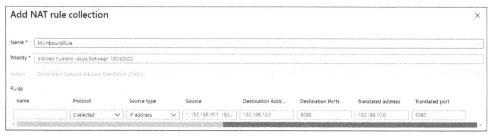

FIGURE 3-13   Azure Firewall DNAT Rule Collection

DNAT rule collections have the following options:

- **Name**   This is a unique name for the collection—up to 80 characters long—which can be used to include relevant information used for rule auditing over time.

- **Priority**   Number from 100 to 65,000 that specifies which order the collection is processed. Lower numbers are processed first. It is advised that you space out rule collection priority so new collections can be inserted between existing ones as needed.

Individual DNAT rules have the following properties:

- **Name**   This is a unique name within the rule.

- **Protocol**   The protocol can be set to TCP or UDP. Multiselect is also allowed.

- **Source Type**   The source type can be either IP Address or IP Group. IP Groups are extremely useful in this context because they can be managed separately from the rules that use them, enabling IP Groups to be dynamic without having to constantly change Firewall configuration.

- **Source**   Sources can be a comma-separated list of IP addresses and CIDR blocks, *, or a multiselect list of IP Groups, if that is the type.

- **Destination Address**   This is a single Azure Firewall associated public IP address that will listen for incoming requests.

- **Destination Port**   A single port to open on the public IP address.

- **Translated Address**   This will be the internal IP address of the resource on the network that will be accessible from the internet.

- **Translated Port**   This will be the destination port on the internal address, which can be different from the public port that is open.

DNAT rules serve a valid purpose, but they should be used with caution. Even though Azure Firewall stands between potential attackers and the resources advertised by the rules, those resources are still vulnerable to attack from the allowed destinations. Whenever possible, restrict the allowed sources to trusted IP ranges and always use strong access control on the destination service.

If DNAT is being used to allow inbound RDP or SSH connections to a jump server, consider using Just-In-Time Access via Azure Security Center. This feature requires users to authenticate to the Azure portal and creates temporary DNAT rules on Azure Firewall to allow access. Learn more at *https://aka.ms/AzNSBook/JIT*.

Rule processing

When traffic is routed to Azure Firewall, it processes the traffic against the configured rule collections in a specific order to determine what action to take.

DNAT rules are technically applied to traffic first, but traffic matching these rules should not be relevant to other rule types. The only overlap is that DNAT rules require network access from the Firewall to the translated address, but this is handled automatically by an implicit network rule created by default to allow traffic.

For traffic originating from internal addresses, network rules are applied before application rules. Since rules are terminating, this means that if a match is found in a network rule, Allow or Deny, this will be the result even if application rules state otherwise. For example, if a network rule is set to Deny an IP address or range, traffic is denied even if there is an application rule allowing the traffic to the corresponding FQDN. The full rule processing order is visualized in Figure 3-14.

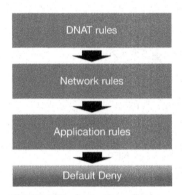

FIGURE 3-14 Azure Firewall rule processing order

Within each rule collection, rules are processed in the order of lowest priority first until a match is found, at which time the configured Action for the rule is performed. If no matches are found in any rule collection, traffic is evaluated against a hidden infrastructure rule collection, which contains FQDNs for some internal infrastructure services. If still no match has been found, traffic is denied.

Azure Firewall Manager

Azure Firewall Manager is a separate Azure resource that is intended to provide a centrally managed layer of security in the hub of a hub-and-spoke network. The hub can be either a VNet that is peered to multiple spokes, as has been the example in this chapter so far, or it could be an Azure Virtual WAN (VWAN) Hub. In either case, Firewall Manager has the ability to centrally manage network security across multiple hubs, whether they are secured with Azure Firewall or by a third-party partnered service, which is possible in VWAN Secured Virtual Hubs.

Firewall policies

Firewall policies are the resource that allows for central management of multiple Azure Firewalls across an environment. A Firewall policy contains various Firewall settings, along with the full ruleset, and can be applied to one or many Azure Firewalls. An example diagram showing central management of Firewall Policies is shown in Figure 3-15.

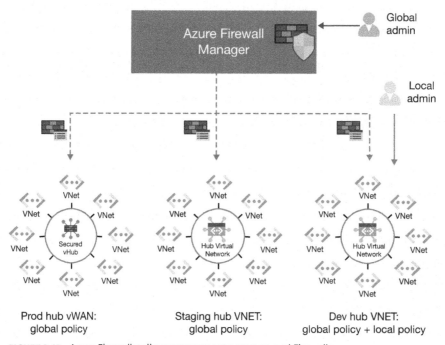

FIGURE 3-15 Azure Firewall policy management across several Firewalls

To use Firewall policies, Firewall Manager must be used to do one of the following:

- Provision an Azure Firewall in a VWAN hub (converting it to a secured virtual hub)

- Convert an existing Firewall in a VNet to be managed by Firewall Manager (known as a hub virtual network)

These processes are covered in the "Hub virtual networks" and "Secured virtual hubs" sections later in this chapter.

The most important thing to note about Firewall policies is that they are a separate entity entirely from the Firewalls they apply to. This has some advantages, including the following:

- One-to-many relationship of Firewall policies to Firewalls. This has a big impact of the scalability of managing many firewalls.

- Resource-level RBAC can be applied to the policy rather than the Firewall. The idea here is that there could be a separation of duties between groups allowed to manage the infrastructure of the firewall and groups that control the rules and other security features.

The difference is shown in Figure 3-16, which compares the configuration options available on a standalone Firewall to the options available on a Firewall converted to be managed by Firewall Manager.

FIGURE 3-16 Azure Firewall standalone versus Azure Firewall managed by Firewall Manager Firewall policies

The same thing can be seen when looking at the ARM templates for the two Firewalls; rather than being part of the Azure Firewall object, the rules, DNS configuration, and threat intelligence configuration are all part of the Firewall Policy, which is a separate object that is related to the Firewall object.

The configuration of threat intelligence remains exactly as it was when the setting was part of the Firewall, but as part of a Firewall Policy, it needs to be configured only once and applies to many Firewalls. The same is true for DNS settings.

Rules and their processing change slightly when using Firewall policy. Most of the concepts remain the same, so those points will not be repeated in this section. For example, the options available for each rule type remain the same, but the interface is changed to a single interface as pictured in Figure 3-17.

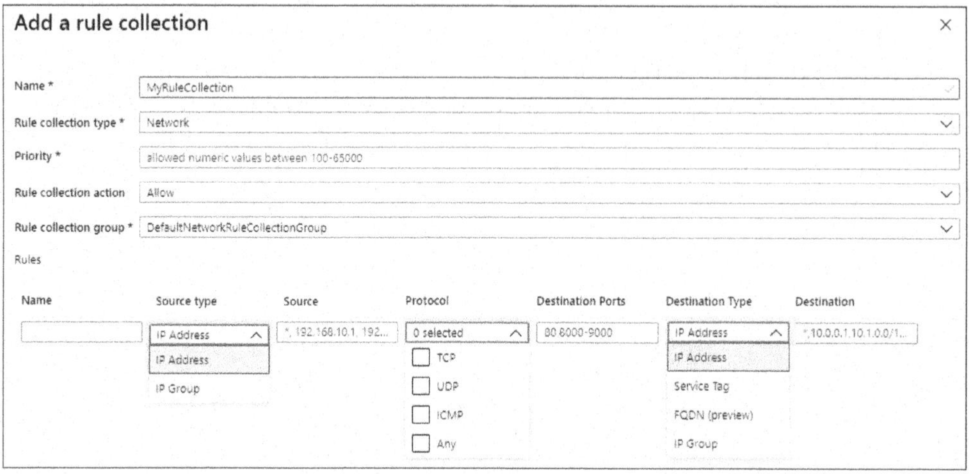

FIGURE 3-17   Azure Firewall policy rule collection properties

All other options are the same as those explained in the "Rule types" section earlier in this chapter, with the exception of rule collection group. This option is only present when using Firewall Policy, and the only option is the default group for each rule type. The significance of this group can be seen in the Rules blade, which is shown in Figure 3-18 and displays the priority of each of the groups (which is the same as described in the earlier "Rule processing" section).

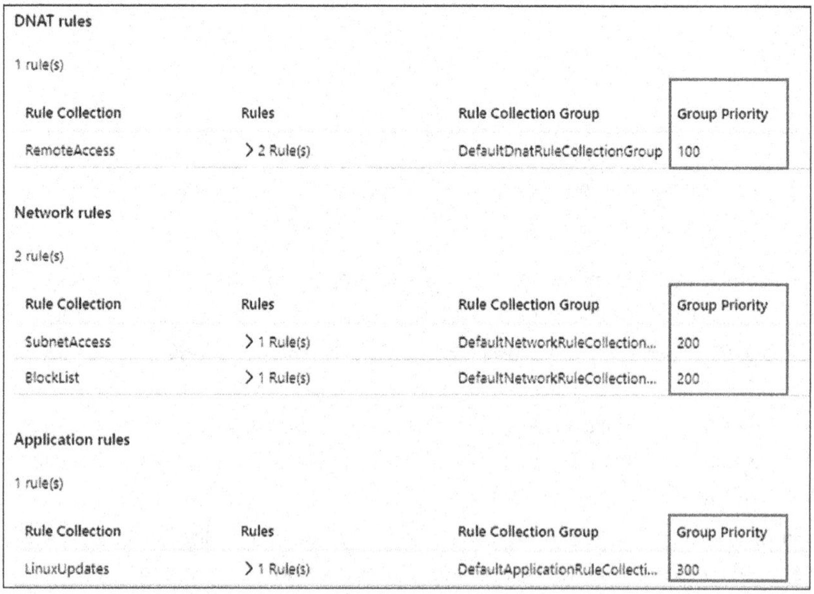

FIGURE 3-18   Azure Firewall rule collection group priority

Rules in each collection have the same options as on a standalone Firewall. The only major difference in rule creation and processing is the addition of the Rule Inheritance option, which is shown in Figure 3-19.

FIGURE 3-19 Azure Firewall policy rule inheritance

Rule Inheritance allows the specification of a parent policy, which is processed first when it comes time to match traffic against rules. This is used when there are central network security standards that must be applied across all environments and Firewalls while allowing for local additions to accommodate specific workloads. For example, a company may allow a common set of FQDNs on the internet to be accessed globally, but some regions may need to add more specific rules to accommodate the workloads present only in that region.

Hub virtual networks

To manage existing Firewalls deployed in VNets, those Firewalls must be onboarded to Firewall Manager. The process is quick, and the result is the removal of the Firewall rules and other configuration from the Firewall object, which is replaced with equivalent settings in a Firewall policy object.

To start the process of converting an existing Firewall, select **Virtual Networks** from the **Firewall Manager** blade and select either **Migrate with a new Firewall Policy** or **Migrate with an existing Firewall Policy**. The Firewall Manager interface is shown in Figure 3-20.

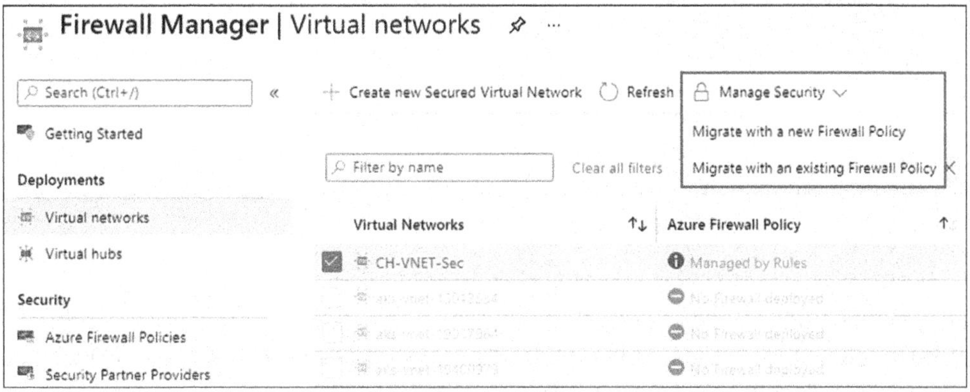

FIGURE 3-20 Azure Firewall hub virtual network conversion

There is also the option to create a new VNet with a Firewall in the same process, which is similar to the process of creating any VNet. With the information provided earlier in this chapter, this should be a familiar process. The conversion process includes the ability to use an existing Azure Firewall from the selected VNet or to create a new Firewall in the VNet.

An additional way to initiate the conversion process is directly from the Firewall. If a Firewall is not already managed by Firewall Manager, there will be a banner on top of the **Overview** page showing the option to manage the Firewall using Firewall Manager, as shown in Figure 3-21.

FIGURE 3-21 Azure Firewall option to manage with Firewall Manager

Whichever method is used to convert or deploy a new Firewall managed by Firewall Manager, the result will be that Firewall policies will be able to be managed separately from Azure Firewalls.

Secured virtual hubs

Secured virtual hubs is the name given to Azure VWAN hubs with an instance of Azure Firewall deployed and managed by Firewall Manager with Firewall policies. Azure VWAN is not discussed in depth in this book, but you can find more information at *https://aka.ms/AzNSBook/ VirtualWAN*. Think of VWAN as a managed hub network that manages much of the routing and connectivity automatically.

To create or convert an existing VWAN hub to a secured virtual hub, use the options in the **Firewall Manager** blade, which is shown in Figure 3-22.

FIGURE 3-22 Azure Firewall Manager secured virtual hubs

The deployment process for Azure Firewall in VWAN hubs is similar enough to deploying in a VNet, so we don't need to demonstrate the full process again. What should be understood here is that the function of Azure Firewall and Firewall Manager is the same whether the deployment is done in a VWAN hub or VNet.

The decision of whether to deploy hubs using the traditional VNet architecture or to use Azure VWAN is one that depends on several factors. The general concept that differs between the approaches is that VNets tend to offer users more control over the network components at the expense of higher management overhead, whereas VWAN hubs provide more automation at the expense of configurability. To research the other factors that go into making the decision between VNets and VWAN hubs, visit *https://aka.ms/AzNSBook/Hubs*.

Third-party security services

Available only in secured virtual hubs (VWAN), Firewall Manager supports the ability to integrate with a third-party security service to inspect traffic. This architecture is commonly used in environments where user traffic is sent through the hub, such as in branch office connectivity or virtual desktop infrastructure environments.

At the time of writing, the three different providers that are supported are Zscaler, iboss, and Check Point. When configured for use in the secured virtual hub, internet-bound traffic is routed to the chosen provider over a VPN gateway. Azure Firewall can also be deployed in the hub to control the traffic inside the network. The diagram in Figure 3-23 shows how this architecture looks.

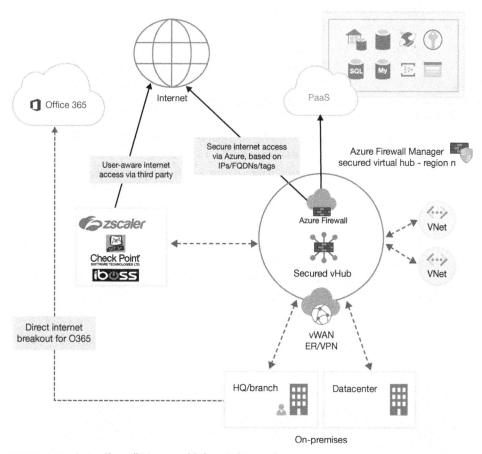

FIGURE 3-23 Azure Firewall Manager third-party integration

The architecture made available by using third-party providers in a secured virtual hub is somewhat similar to what could be manually set up using forced tunneling with Azure Firewall deployed in a VNet, but Azure VWAN handles much of the configuration work automatically.

The Azure Firewall in this architecture is managed by Firewall Manager, including the ability to use Firewall policies alongside other Firewalls deployed in the environment.

The end goal of using both Azure Firewall and a third-party provider is to take advantage of the platform-native services for most traffic and forward traffic from user environments that requires additional inspection to purpose-built services that specialize in this type of traffic inspection.

Summary

Network segmentation is a very important component of network security. Whether in VWAN secured virtual hubs or in hub VNets, Azure Firewall can exist in several different architectures to provide secure connectivity by controlling traffic for segmentation.

Centralization is a key component to using Azure Firewall for segmentation of traffic, and that centralization includes both the management component and the logging of Firewall activities and traffic. Using Firewall Manager to manage multiple Firewalls is recommended to keep environments standardized, and using Azure Monitor to centralize logs in Log Analytics is recommended for comprehensive visibility.

The information provided in this chapter should provide you with a foundation of knowledge about Azure Firewall and Firewall Manager to integrate the tools into a secure Azure environment. Using these resources in combination with the other Azure components detailed throughout the book is the focus of Chapter 9.

## Chapter 4

Traffic Inspection in Azure Networks

Security teams often require a deeper level of visibility than the standard traffic logs generated by Azure Firewall, NSGs, and other resources. This deeper level of visibility can take many forms, and native Azure resources can accomplish many of the requirements. Traffic inspection, or Deep Packet Inspection, refers to the ability to inspect the entire packet, rather than just the headers, of a request.

Traffic inspection generally has a few main components:

- **Decryption**   Encrypted traffic, such as TLS, must be decrypted before any inspection can be done.

- **Inspection**   Traffic can be inspected using several methodologies, including Intrusion Detection and Prevention Systems (IDPS), Data Loss Prevention (DLP), Anti-malware, and others.

- **Logging and Capture**   Some components of inspected and decrypted traffic can be logged using the standard mechanisms. Full packet capture feeds are also possible in some scenarios.

Currently in Azure, some elements of each of the previous components of traffic inspection are available. For inbound web application traffic, Azure WAF performs all three functions and will be covered in Chapter 5, "Secure application delivery with Azure Web Application Firewall." For other network traffic, or in addition to WAF, there are other options available in Azure. Azure Firewall Premium can now decrypt traffic, inspect it with a built-in IDPS engine, and log the resulting data. For full packet capture, Azure Network Watcher can enable packet capture on target virtual machines.

Azure Firewall Premium

Azure Firewall Premium is the latest offering based on the same technology platform as Azure Firewall, but it has some important upgraded features. Azure Firewall Premium was developed for customers who want to make use of cloud-native network resources and also take advantage of more advanced security features.

The Premium SKU of Azure Firewall represents an evolution of the proven cloud-native firewall technology toward a set of capabilities that more closely approximates what Next-Generation Firewalls are capable of. By using Azure Firewall Premium, organizations can now more confidently use the native Azure offering as a primary part of their security stack without relying on third-party NVAs.

Introducing Azure Firewall Premium

Azure Firewall Standard has been generally available since September 2018. It is a cloud-native firewall-as-a-service offering that enables customers to centrally govern and log all their traffic flows using a DevOps approach. The service supports both application and network-level filtering rules and is integrated with the Microsoft Threat Intelligence feed for filtering known malicious IP addresses and domains. Azure Firewall is highly available with built-in autoscaling.

Although Azure Firewall Standard has been a good fit for many customer scenarios, it is lacking key next-generation firewall capabilities that are required for highly sensitive and regulated environments. Azure Firewall Premium is Azure's first step toward closing these gaps.

The main features included in Azure Firewall Premium are

- **TLS termination**   Because a majority of traffic today is encrypted, being able to terminate traffic and inspect it is a key feature for detecting threats inside your network. It also gives more granular control to enforce destination URL filtering.

- **IDS/IPS integration**   Conjoined with TLS termination, intrusion detection and prevention capabilities provide a first layer of defense against known attacks. Threat feeds update regularly to protect the network from emerging threats.

- **Web categories**   For better management and enforcement of web traffic, customers can define rules based on web categories, excluding high-risk categories such as gambling or approving certain categories for organization's wide use, while leveraging the granularity of URL filtering.

As the service matures, Firewall Premium is expected to support additional security scenarios such as DLP, malware detection, and advanced anomaly detection.

Ido Frizler, Principal group manager, Azure Networking team

Deploying Azure Firewall Premium

Azure Firewall Premium is an altogether separate resource from the standard version of Azure Firewall because some of the advanced features require more processing power, and therefore, different back-end resources are used. For this reason, there is currently no upgrade path from Azure Firewall to Azure Firewall Premium.

Azure Firewall Premium can be deployed using the same wizard that is used to create a standard Azure Firewall. Figure 4-1 shows the Firewall creation process with the configuration items specific to Azure Firewall Premium highlighted.

FIGURE 4-1 The Azure Firewall creation wizard with the Premium options highlighted

It is important to notice that when you select Premium, you must use a Firewall Policy to manage the firewall, rather than rules directly configured on the Firewall. All new features will be rolled out to Firewall Policy, so this should be chosen for any new deployments. Figure 4-2 shows the policy creation process from the resource creation wizard. Note that the Policy Tier must be set to Premium to use all the features included in Azure Firewall Premium.

FIGURE 4-2 Creating a Firewall Policy as part of the Azure Firewall creation wizard

TLS inspection

You can configure Azure Firewall Premium to terminate outbound TLS traffic so inspection techniques, such as IDPS and URL filtering, can be used. The method used to inspect traffic is similar to a man-in-the-middle attack in that the source system is unaware that their communication to a remote site is not private. This is accomplished by manipulating certificate trust to create an extra connection between the source and destination.

When you configure Azure Firewall Premium to terminate TLS connections, it will trick the source system into communicating with it instead of the intended destination. To do this, Firewall needs to use a certificate that the source endpoint trusts to replace the original certificate presented by the destination. When configured for TLS Termination, the firewall acts as a subordinate or intermediate Certification Authority (CA), which is issuing website certificates on behalf of a Root CA that is trusted by the clients.

Certificates can come from many places, including a public certification authority, a private key infrastructure (PKI), such as Active Directory Certificate Services, or even a self-signed certificate from any computer. The origin of the certificate is less important than configuring client machines to trust it. This certificate trust can be established using some common methods, including the following:

- **Deploy with automation** This option works well in nondomain environments where there are existing servers that need to be configured to trust a new CA—in this case, the firewall impersonating a CA. Scripts can be run to add the certificate to the Trusted Root Certification Authorities certificate store of any machine that will be subject to TLS Inspection.

- **Custom images**   If VMs are frequently rebuilt from image, or if TLS Inspection is being set up in a newly built environment, it may make sense to embed the configuration in the OS image. This mechanism only works if machines get rebuilt periodically or another method needs to be chosen to update expiring or replaced certificates.

- **Enterprise CA**   In Active Directory environments that use PKI to manage certificates, this process is the simplest. When an Enterprise CA exists within a domain, all domain-joined machines automatically trust the Root CA and all certificates signed by it or its subordinate CAs.

Certificate creation using Active Directory Certificate Services

When an enterprise CA generates the certificate used by Azure Firewall Premium to perform TLS Inspection, no extra configuration is needed on domain-joined clients to trust the certificate. For this reason, this section covers the process used to generate a subordinate CA certificate from an enterprise CA.

The goal of the following process is to generate a .pfx file containing a subordinate CA certificate along with its key. This certificate and key combination is used by Azure Firewall Premium to reissue website certificates to clients after terminating the initial client connection and making the request on behalf of the client. Acting as the man in the middle enables the firewall to log and inspect traffic in its unencrypted state.

To request and export the proper certificate, use the following steps:

1. Navigate to the Active Directory Certificate Services enrollment website on an Enterprise CA, usually *https://<servername>/certsrv* and select **Request a Certificate**.

2. Choose **Advanced Certificate Request**.

3. Choose **Create And Submit A Request To This CA**.

4. Fill out the form using the Subordinate Certification Authority, as shown in Figure 4-3.

5. Submit the request and install the certificate.

6. Assuming this request has been made from a Windows server using Internet Explorer, open **Internet Options**.

7. Navigate to the **Content** tab and select **Certificates**.

8. Select the certificate that was just issued and click **Export**.

9. Click **Next** to begin the wizard, then click **Yes**, export the private key, and click **Next**.

10. For file format, .pfx is selected by default. Deselect the box for **Include All Certificates In The Certification Path If Possible**.

11. Assign and confirm a password to protect the key and click **Next**.

12. Choose a file name and export location and click **Next**.

13. Click **Finish** and move the exported certificate to a secure location.

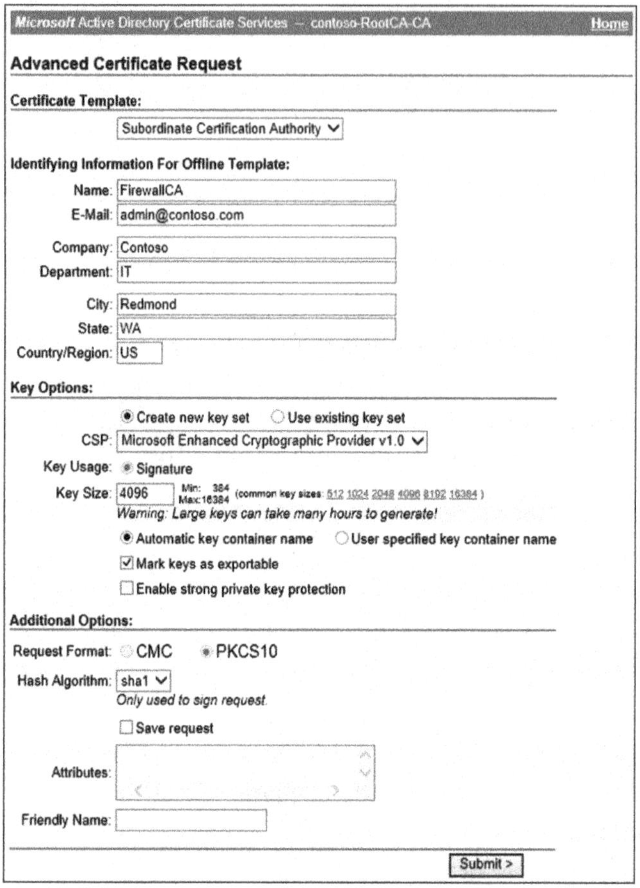

FIGURE 4-3 An Active Directory Certification Services certificate request

Configuring Azure Firewall for TLS Inspection

Once a certificate has been created for Azure Firewall Premium to use, the next prerequisites that must exist are a key vault to store the certificate in and a managed identity for the firewall to use to access the certificate. The certificate must be added to a key vault, as shown in Figure 4-4.

Create a certificate

Method of Certificate Creation

| Import | ∨ |

Certificate Name * ⓘ

| AzFirewallSubCA |

Upload Certificate File *

| "AzFirewallSubCA.pfx" | 🖩 |

Password

| •••••••• | ⓟ |

Create

FIGURE 4-4   The Key Vault Create/Import process

You can add the necessary information to the TLS Inspection blade in the Firewall Policy as Figure 4-5 depicts.

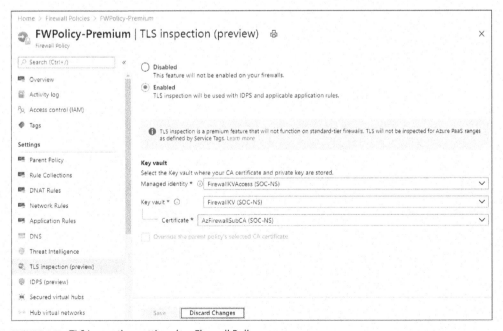

FIGURE 4-5   TLS Inspection settings in a Firewall Policy

After the settings have been configured, Azure Firewall Premium begins performing TLS Inspection on any outbound traffic that matches an application rule that is configured for inspection. See the upcoming section, "Using full URL for traffic management," for details. This section also contains instructions for how to validate that TLS Inspection is working correctly.

Intrusion detection and prevention

Intrusion detection and prevention systems (IDPS) inspect traffic by comparing observed traffic against signatures of known malicious traffic. If traffic matches signatures, it can either be logged (detection) or blocked (prevention).

Some systems, which offer only detection and not prevention, ingest a copy of network traffic to analyze rather than analyzing live traffic in real time. These systems use the passive form of IDS inspection, which is not able to block any malicious traffic because it only sees a copy of the traffic. This approach can be advantageous in environments with lower risk profiles or where the need for availability and low latency is a higher priority than real-time prevention.

Azure Firewall Premium uses the inline form of IDS, which means that the detection engine acts in real-time because it sits in the traffic path. Being inline allows Azure Firewall Premium to move beyond IDS and into IDPS because it can block traffic that matches signatures.

You configure IDPS settings in the IDPS blade of the Firewall Policy. Figure 4-6 shows the IDPS Mode settings, which are

- **Disabled**   When disabled, no traffic inspection is done.
- **Alert**   Alert mode writes logs to the AzureFirewallIDSLog OperationName in Log Analytics.
- **Alert And Deny**   This setting denies traffic along with writing logs when rules are matched.

FIGURE 4-6   IDPS mode options

Tuning the IDPS ruleset may be necessary if false positives are encountered during testing. The ruleset used by Azure Firewall Premium is managed, meaning that rules are selected based on their fidelity and enabled by default. When it becomes necessary to change the behavior of any rules, you can do this in the Signature Rules tab, as shown in Figure 4-7.

FIGURE 4-7 Mode options of IDPS Signature Rules

The procedure to test IDPS signatures for false positives starts with running the IDPS engine in Alert mode for some period of time as the Firewall is subjected to normal traffic patterns. A good range to start with is 14 to 30 days, but the optimal period of time to use detection mode depends on the volume and quality of traffic. As traffic passes through the Firewall and is inspected, any signature matches are logged. You can find the resulting data in Log Analytics using the following query:

```
AzureDiagnostics
| where ResourceType == "AZUREFIREWALLS"
| where OperationName == "AzureFirewallIDSLog"
```

A sample IDPS match log is shown in Figure 4-8.

TenantId	
TimeGenerated [UTC]	2021-02-03T05:1b09.687Z
ResourceId	/SUBSCRIPTIONS/ /RESOURCEGROUPS/ /PROVIDERS/MICROSOFT.NETWORK/AZUREFIREWALLS/AZFIREWALLPREMIUM
Category	AzureFirewallNetworkRule
ResourceGroup	
SubscriptionId	
ResourceProvider	MICROSOFT.NETWORK
Resource	AZFIREWALLPREMIUM
ResourceType	AZUREFIREWALLS
OperationName	AzureFirewallIDSLog
SourceSystem	Azure
msg_s	TCP request from 10.10.20.4:4293 to 10.10.30.4:80 Action: alert. Signature: 2008983. IDS: USER_AGENTS Suspicious User Agent (BlackSun). Priority: 1. Classification: A Network Trojan was detected
Type	AzureDiagnostics
_ResourceId	/subscriptions/ /resourcegroups/ providers/microsoft.network/azurefirewalls/azfirewallpremium

FIGURE 4-8 An IDS rule match log in Log Analytics

As matches are accumulated and determined to be false positives, not actual malicious activity, the signature ID can be set to either Alert or Disabled to prevent false positive matches from being blocked. Once the testing period has elapsed, the IDPS Mode should be set to Alert and Deny.

Another method of tuning the IDPS signatures is to create Bypass rules. The Bypass List enables you to create granular rules, which, when matched, exempt traffic from all IDPS inspection. Rather than disabling a signature globally, it could be less risky to simply bypass the exact conditions under which false positives occur. Figure 4-9 illustrates some examples.

IDPS mode	Signature rules	**Bypass list**							
IDPS will not filter traffic to any of the IP addresses, ranges, and subnets specified below.									
Name	Source type	Source	Protocol	Port	Destination ty...	Destination		Inherited from	
BypassSource	IP Address	10.5.1.0/24	ANY	*	IP Address	*			🗑 ...
BypassDestination	IP Address	*	ANY	*	IP Address	10.6.8.10			🗑 ...
BypassSpecific	IP Address	10.45.3.0/24	TCP	8080	IP Group	LinuxServers			🗑 ...
	IP Address ∧	*, 192.168.10.1, 192.168.10.0...	∧	80,8000-9000	IP Address ∧	*, 192.168.10.1, 192.168.10.0/			
	IP Address		TCP		IP Address				
	IP Group		UDP		IP Group				
			ICMP						
			ANY						

FIGURE 4-9 A Bypass List in IDPS settings

The IDPS engine of Azure Firewall Premium inspects all traffic passed through the Firewall, but it is important to note that not all signatures are processed for every direction of traffic. For instance, some signatures only apply to outbound or east-west traffic. When TLS Inspection is configured, the IDPS engine also has the ability to inspect decrypted outbound HTTPS traffic as it passes. Because Azure Firewall Premium does not perform TLS Inspection on inbound traffic, Azure WAF, which is discussed in Chapter 5, should be used to inspect inbound web application traffic.

Using full URLs for traffic management

As discussed in Chapter 3, "Controlling traffic with Azure Firewall," Azure Firewall Standard can be configured to manage outbound traffic using application rules. Because most internet-bound web traffic is encrypted using TLS, only the FQDN of the destination can be seen. This is a limiting factor in terms of how granular traffic filtering rules can be.

With Azure Firewall Premium, TLS Inspection can be configured for outbound traffic, which opens up new options for traffic filtering. Instead of relying on just FQDN-based rules, you can configure application rules in Premium Firewall policies using full URLs. This added granularity provides a more secure option for allowing outbound traffic because the precise endpoint can be specified without needing to open access to an entire FQDN. Some examples are shown in Figure 4-10.

Name *	Source type	Source	Protocol *	TLS inspection	Destination Type *	Destination *	
MSFT	IP Address ∨	10.0.1.0/24	Http:80,Https:443	☑ TLS inspection	URL ∨	microsoft.com/en-us/download/developer-tools.aspx,github.com/azure*	🗑 ...
Search	IP Address	10.0.1.0/24	Http:80,Https:443	☐ TLS inspection	FQDN	*google.com,*bing.com	🗑 ...

FIGURE 4-10 An application rule collection with TLS inspection and URL destinations

You also can use TLS Inspection and full URL filtering with web categories. These categories are provided as a Microsoft managed feed as part of both Azure Firewall Standard and Premium. The major difference between using web categories on each Firewall type is that when used with Premium, they can be combined with TLS Inspection to take advantage of a more granular list of URL categories. Azure Firewall Standard uses FQDN categories.

The categories available are broken down into groups as shown in Table 4-1.

TABLE 4-1 Azure Firewall web categories

Liability	High-Bandwidth	Business Use	Productivity Loss	General Surfing
Alcohol and tobacco	Image sharing	Business	Advertisements and pop-ups	Arts
Child abuse images	Peer-to-peer	Computers and technology	Chat	Fashion and beauty
Child inappropriate	Streaming media and downloads	Education	Cults	General Greeting cards
Criminal activity	Download sites	Finance	Games	Leisure and recreation
Dating and personals	Entertainment	Forums and newsgroups	Instant messaging	Nature and conservation
Gambling			Shopping	Politics
Hacking		Government	Social networking	Real estate
Hate and intolerance		Health and medicine		Religion
Illegal drug		Information security		Restaurants and dining
Illegal software		Job search		Sports
Lingerie and swimsuits		News		Transportation
Marijuana		Non-profits and NGOs		Travel
Nudity		Personal sites		
Pornography/sexually explicit		Private IP addresses		
School cheating		Professional networking		
Self-harm		Search engines and portals		
Sex education		Translators		
Tasteless		File Repository		
Violence		Web-based email		
Weapons				

There are two broad examples of how URL categories tend to be used:

- **Allow List** In more secure environments, Azure Firewall's Default Deny policy ensures that only traffic that is specifically allowed via rules is permitted. Web categories can supplement existing FQDN- or URL-based allow lists in cases where it is too difficult to manage a long list of individual URLs or FQDNs. An example of this is shown in Figure 4-11.

FIGURE 4-11 An application rule collection using web category destinations

- **Block List** There are some workloads that run in Azure that are expected to have more permissive internet access, and for these environments, it may be difficult, if not impossible, to manage an allow list. For these situations, the Default Deny behavior of Azure Firewall can be overridden by an "allow all" application rule, which should be given the lowest possible priority. As shown in Figure 4-12, deny rule collections can then be created at higher priority using a combination of web categories, URLs, and FQDNs.

FIGURE 4-12 An Application Rule collection allowing all traffic except blocked categories

Note that the Block List model is recommended only for environments containing Windows Virtual Desktop or other workloads primarily used by end users. This is a very permissive setup compared to the Allow List model, which should always be used in server environments and others that need tighter security.

Validating TLS inspection

Once the TLS inspection settings are in place on the firewall and the root CA certificate is trusted on clients, you can verify that termination is working as expected by checking both client behavior and logging.

To determine whether traffic is being inspected from a client, log into a VM that is subject to an application rule configured for TLS inspection and browse to an allowed destination. The connection should be allowed, and there should be no certificate warnings for the TLS connection. The only way to find a clue that the connection was terminated by the firewall is by checking the site security details in the browser, as shown in Figure 4-13.

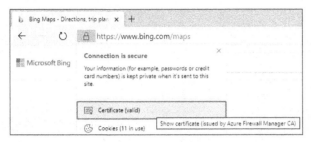

FIGURE 4-13 Browser security details

Showing the certificate reveals more details, including the certificate chain leading back to the trusted root CA, in this case the enterprise CA that is trusted automatically by all domain clients. Figure 4-14 shows the complete certificate details.

FIGURE 4-14 TLS Inspection certificate details

Another way to verify that TLS Inspection is functioning properly is to check the log output from the rules. Run the following query in Log Analytics to find all Application Rule logs containing full URL paths:

```
AzureDiagnostics
| where ResourceType == "AZUREFIREWALLS"
| where Category == "AzureFirewallApplicationRule"
| where msg_s contains "Url:"
| sort by TimeGenerated desc
```

A sample log generated by a request matching a TLS inspection application rule is shown in Figure 4-15, including the full URL of the request.

TenantId	0f992c69-
TimeGenerated [UTC]	2021-02-04T04:33:14.245Z
ResourceId	/SUBSCRIPTIONS/1C61CCBF- /RESOURCEGROUPS/ /PROVIDERS/MICROSOFT.NETWORK/AZUREFIREWALLS/AZFIREWALLPREMIUM
Category	AzureFirewallApplicationRule
ResourceGroup	
SubscriptionId	1c61ccbf-
ResourceProvider	MICROSOFT.NETWORK
Resource	AZFIREWALLPREMIUM
ResourceType	AZUREFIREWALLS
OperationName	AzureFirewallApplicationRuleLog
SourceSystem	Azure
msg_s	HTTP request from 10.10.20.4:20015 to www.msftconnecttest.com:80 Url: www.msftconnecttest.com/connecttest.txt. Action: Deny. No rule matched. Proceeding with default action
Type	AzureDiagnostics
_ResourceId	/subscriptions/1c61ccbf- /resourcegroups/ providers/microsoft.network/azurefirewalls/azfirewallpremium

FIGURE 4-15   Full URL details in application rule logs

Network Watcher packet capture

There are some situations that require security or operations teams to have a full copy of network communications in the form of a packet capture. For example, if a machine is suspected to be compromised, remotely initiating a packet capture is a good way to gather additional data for an investigation.

Network Watcher is capable of running packet capture on Azure virtual machines for a set period of time and storing the resulting data locally on the machine, in Azure Storage, or both. At the time of this book's publication, this is the only native way to generate a packet capture. There is currently no method available to capture network traffic more broadly than an individual VM. The VNet TAP preview is currently on hold but is expected to be available again in the future. See *https://aka.ms/AzNSBook/VNetTAP* for updates.

The packet capture process is initiated using Network Watcher. It is recommended that you use the following process at least once for every virtual machine environment to ensure that prerequisites are met and that subsequent captures run quickly and without issue.

If capture files will be written to a storage account, the VM must have access to the storage endpoint. When a capture is initiated for the first time, a network watcher is created in the region where the VM is deployed and the AzureNetworkWatcherExtension VM extension is installed automatically. Doing this ahead of time speeds up the process of initiating captures in the future because the prerequisites will be in place already.

Figure 4-16 shows the options for creating a packet capture, which is a process that must be followed for each virtual machine to be monitored. The packet capture process is not ongoing and has a time limit of five hours, so this process must be completed anytime packet capture is necessary. We show the process using the Azure portal, but you can do it using CLI, API, or ARM.

FIGURE 4-16 The options available when creating a packet capture.

The process to initiate a packet capture via the Azure Portal follows:

1. Navigate to **Network Watcher → Packet Capture** and select **Add**.

2. Select the **Subscription**, **Resource Group**, and **VM** to create a capture on; then give the capture a name.

3. Select where to store the capture file (.cap format). If you select a Storage account, one must already exist. When choosing a local file, specify the path.

4. Optionally set the values for **Maximum Bytes Per Packet**, **Maximum Bytes Per Session**, and **Time Limit**. The default values are all set to the maximum allowed.

5. Optionally add one or more filters. Each filter can contain values for **Protocol**, **Local IP Address**, **Local Port**, **Remote IP Address**, and **Remote Port**. Filters can have a big impact on the size of the capture file but could leave out relevant data.

Once the capture is created, you can check the status in Network Watcher as shown in Figure 4-17.

FIGURE 4-17 Packet capture in progress

When a packet capture finishes, the file or files generated are located in the destinations configured in the capture settings. There will be a link to the storage location of the capture file in the details of the finished capture, as shown in Figure 4-18.

FIGURE 4-18 The details of a completed packet capture

Clicking the link to the storage location takes you to the file location, where you can download the file for analysis, as shown in Figure 4-19. If a local file location was also specified in the capture settings, the same file can also be retrieved from the VM if necessary.

FIGURE 4-19 The storage location of the capture file

The capture file contains a record of all network communication to and from the virtual machine, subject to the configured filters. There are many methods available to read and analyze the data. Wireshark is the most common tool used to read and filter capture files if manual analysis is required. There is an excellent document available to apply some of the same IDS principles discussed earlier in the chapter to capture data. See *https://aka.ms/AzNSBook/ CaptureIDS* for a guide to building an open-source passive IDS to analyze VM packet capture data.

Summary

This chapter has introduced the current methods available to do deep packet inspection in Azure networks, Azure Firewall Premium, and Network Watcher. Whatever the method used, the goal is to gain the deepest level of visibility into network traffic.

Azure Firewall Premium is now able to terminate outbound TLS connections to perform granular traffic filtering and inspection with IDPS signatures. Performing traffic inspection at the central point in the network ensures that all traffic is subject to some inspection, and that this inspection is continuous. Network Watcher can supplement this central inspection with on-demand endpoint packet captures, which are a great asset when performing forensic investigation.

## Chapter 5

Secure application delivery with Azure Web Application Firewall

This book is supposed to be about network security, but this chapter is about application security. The two concepts are unique, but they are so intertwined that they often cannot be discussed separately. Web applications are accessed via public and private networks, and the back-end components that make up those applications exist on networks as well. Network and application security can face different threats that exploit different vulnerabilities, but the tools used to address the security of each need to work together, so are best understood together.

A Web Application Firewall (WAF) is a security component that inspects inbound traffic to web applications (Layer 7) to detect and prevent attacks. WAF is not the same thing as a firewall, which is traditionally focused on Layers 3 and 4. Firewalls usually also have some application layer capabilities, but this is not the primary focus.

It is important to understand that a WAF is not meant to be the only layer of defense against web application attacks. Application code, network connections, and databases all play a role in the security of an application, but no single part can assume the full burden of protecting the confidentiality, integrity, and availability of the application. Not every organization has the means to ensure applications are always completely free from vulnerability to exploit, so WAF exists as an extra layer of defense.

Azure WAF has the ability to detect and prevent common web application attacks, including common and effective attacks such as SQL injection and cross-site scripting, known bot activity, and a host of other possible attacks via custom rules. It is recommended that this extra layer of security be applied to any web application, especially those that are publicly accessible.

The need for Azure WAF

Cyber criminals frequently target web applications and APIs to steal customer data and user credentials and to cause the denial of service. A successful web attack could cause serious damage to a victim, both financially and in brand reputation. Many organizations mandate a web application firewall (WAF) to be placed in front of all public-facing web applications to comply with regulatory requirements and to protect web applications from targeted nonvolumetric and volumetric denial of service attacks.

Azure WAF offers a managed preconfigured ruleset against Open Source Foundation for Application Security Project (OWASP) vulnerabilities. By default, Azure-managed rulesets are enabled to detect SQL injection (SQLI), Local File Inclusion (LFI), Cross-Site Scripting (XSS), and other common attacks. Managed rulesets support exclusions for specified fields to be ignored during a WAF inspection. Furthermore, for specific scenarios, custom detection and mitigation rules can be defined that are based on a combination of IP address ranges, geolocations, sizes, and http parameters. Azure WAF supports both match rules as well as rate limiting rules. Rate limiting rules restrict the number of requests allowed from any IP address.

Attacks launched by malicious bots surged in the last couple of years since bot nets are now readily available. Azure WAF Bot manager detects and blocks bad bots while allowing good bots access. WAF metrics and logs are natively integrated with Azure monitor, offering real-time visibility into attack insights. Logs can be streamed to customer's SIEM system for centralized security events management. Azure WAF is fully managed by APIs and can easily be integrated with a CI/CD pipeline.

As web application attacks grow in frequency, magnitude, and sophistication, Azure WAF continuously evolves to adapt to new threats for better protection.

Teresa Yao, Principal program manager

Integrating WAF into app delivery architecture

Azure WAF is the name for a common set of capabilities that can be attached to different application delivery services in Azure. WAF can be attached to Application Gateway, Front Door, or CDN (Content Delivery Network). Although there are some differences in capabilities, the core features are common among all services WAF can attach to. To use WAF at the optimal point in the web application architecture, some considerations must be made regarding the architecture of the web application components and the WAF capabilities that will be used.

Load Balancing Options

There are two main types of load balancers available in Azure, each having two different options. The major distinction to understand is between Layer 4 and Layer 7 load balancing. Layer 4 load balancing ignores any application-specific elements of traffic and passes traffic to back-end pool members based only on the UDP/TCP information present. This is different from Layer 7 load balancing in that the latter uses application layer information, such as URL, to pass traffic. To do this, the application load balancing services in Azure also act as the termination point for TLS connections.

The Layer 4 load balancing options include Azure Load Balancer and Azure Traffic Manager. The difference between these services is the scope of the location where they are deployed. Load Balancer is a regional service, which gets deployed to a specific Azure Region or Availability Zone. Traffic Manager is a global service, which means that it is not limited to a particular region but is instead available at any region traffic reaches Azure.

There is a similar distinction between the Layer 7 load balancers: Application Gateway is deployed to a specific region, whereas Front Door is global. There are differences and relative advantages to using either service (or both) to deliver applications, but one thing they have in common is the ability to enable WAF functionality, which is the point of the chapter. As long as either Application Gateway or Front Door is serving as the front end for application traffic, WAF can and should be used.

> **TIP** For more information on selecting the right load balancer for the workload, see *aka.ms/AzNSBook/LoadBalancing.*

Application Gateway

Azure Application Gateway is the regional Layer 7 load balancer offered in Azure. There are two versions of the service, V1 and V2, either of which is capable of integrating WAF. This book focuses specifically on V2, unless otherwise specified. Application Gateway V2 is an autoscaling PaaS service that is deployed in a dedicated subnet within a VNet. It can serve applications internally to the VNet or publicly on the internet.

> **TIP** To learn about the full set of capabilities Application Gateway has, visit *aka.ms/AzNSBook/ApplicationGateway.*

Some common scenarios where Application Gateway is chosen as the application load balancer include the following:

- **Internal-only web applications** Many customers choose Application Gateway to front their private applications because it can be deployed directly in the VNet where the back-end resources reside. When adhering to Zero Trust principles, internal applications can also benefit from the added security that WAF provides.

- **Region-specific public web applications** Some internet-facing web applications only need to be available in certain regions. In some cases, there are requirements that all application components, including the load balancing, be deployed only in certain regions. In these cases, Application Gateway can serve as the only load balancer for the application. In cases where applications need to be available across regions, Azure Front Door can be used.

- **Azure Kubernetes Service (AKS)** Application Gateway natively integrates with AKS and can be deployed as an ingress controller to control inbound traffic to the pods. This can be configured either as an AKS add-on or via Helm. See the full details at *https://aka.ms/AzNSBook/AKS*.

Azure Front Door

Front Door is the global application load balancing service in Azure, which is built for applications that demand availability across regions, along with the scale to handle the largest workloads. Front Door is used for global delivery of services such as XBOX Live, Office 365, and Bing. Front Door is not deployed in a VNet, so is not constrained to any particular region. Rather, the service exists outside the boundary of customer-managed networks and can forward traffic to back ends in Azure or any other location, including other cloud providers or on-premise data centers.

> **TIP** You can find more details on the capabilities of Front Door at
> *https://aka.ms/AzNSBook/FrontDoor*.

In practice, the most common cases when Front Door is chosen as the application load balancer include the following:

- **Multiregion high availability** Some customers are interested in extending their high availability beyond Availability Zones, adding multiple regionally deployed application architectures as back ends of a Front Door. This architecture has the ability to support massive scale and several layers of redundancy for availability.

- **Multi-cloud applications** There are circumstances when application assets are not all running in the same environment, but are spread across either different cloud providers, on-premise datacenters, or some combination of these. Front Door can route traffic to back ends anywhere to support this scenario. Application Gateway also has this ability.

- **Public PaaS back ends** It is increasingly common to build applications using PaaS services that are not bound to a VNet, such as Azure Web Apps and Azure Functions. In these architectures, it can be beneficial to use Front Door over Application Gateway because it does not require any VNet infrastructure.

- **Global application acceleration** Even if the back ends of an application served by Front Door reside in a single region, there is a performance advantage to using Front Door for load balancing. The front-end pool of Azure Front Door sites is made up of every Azure region across the globe, so traffic enters the Azure network at the point closest to the user. This speeds application delivery because traffic is able to traverse the Azure network rather than the public internet for more of the journey.

WAF types

Azure WAF has slightly different capabilities depending on which service it is attached to. The goal is to come closer to offering the same features for every WAF type, but until then, it is helpful to understand the differences present.

The broad distinction between WAF types is between global and regional deployments. Front Door and CDN have roughly equivalent capabilities, and both versions of Application Gateway are very similar, with V2 expanding on the feature set of V1. The main reason for this difference is that WAF is closely integrated with the technology it is attached to; even though the broad capabilities are the same, the particulars vary due to the differences in the underlying platforms.

Front Door and CDN WAF types have different managed rulesets than Application Gateway WAF types. Although they are also based on the ModSec Core Ruleset (CRS), which is also found in the Application Gateway implementation, the active rules represent only a subset of the full list due to some pretuning that has been applied. There will be more discussion of the CRS later in the chapter. Along with the different set of rules, the global WAF also handles rule matching and blocking differently than the regional WAF; regional WAF uses anomaly scoring to block traffic, whereas the global WAF does not. Anomaly scoring is discussed later in this chapter.

Aside from the distinction between Application Gateway V1 and V2, there is also a difference between the concepts of WAF Policy and WAF Configuration. WAF Configuration is the legacy method of managing WAF settings applied directly to the Application Gateway that WAF is applied to. In contrast, a WAF Policy is a separate Azure resource, which is then associated to the Application Gateway (or Front Door or CDN) it is applied to. This can be understood similarly to how Azure Firewall Policy is a separate object from the Firewall (or Firewalls) it is associated with.

The progression of capabilities of the regional Azure WAF on Application Gateway can be summarized by saying that WAF on Application Gateway V2 is more capable than V1, and using WAF Policy over WAF Config provides yet more capabilities. All new WAF features will be rolled out to WAF Policy only, so it is important to move to using WAF Policy rather than Config whenever possible. To learn more about the migration process, see *https://aka.ms/AzNSBook/MigrateWAF*.

The full list of differences among the different WAF types is shown in Figure 5-1. For the purposes of this book, most discussion of WAF centers around WAF Policy because this is the current best practice to deploy and manage Azure WAF. Once the differences of WAF are well understood, you can map security requirements to the capabilities of each.

Feature	WAF Config		WAF Policy		
	Application Gateway V1	Application Gateway V2	Application Gateway V2	Front Door	CDN
OWASP CRS 3.1	✗	✓	✓	✗	✗
OWASP CRS 3.0	✓	✓	✓	✗	✗
OWASP CRS 2.2.9	✓	✓	✓	✗	✗
Microsoft BotManagerRuleSet 0.1	✗	✗	✓	✗	✗
Microsoft BotManagerRuleSet 1.0	✗	✗	✗	✓	✗
DefaultRuleset 1.0	✗	✗	✗	✓	✓
Geo Location Policy	✗	✗	✓	✓	✓
Rate limit Rule	✗	✗	✗	✓	✓
Per-Site Policy	✗	✗	✓	✗	✗
Per-Uri Policy	✗	✗	✓	✗	✗
Custom Policy	✗	PowerShell	GUI	GUI	GUI

FIGURE 5-1   Azure WAF types comparison matrix

WAF deployment

You can deploy WAF very quickly once the application infrastructure, including the application load balancer (Application Gateway or Front Door), is in place. Because this book focuses on security rather than application delivery, the setup of the Front Door and Application Gateway is covered in depth, except for a few prerequisites.

Before deployment

To deploy WAF, you should keep in mind a few prerequisites. An existing application delivery architecture including Application Gateway, Front Door, or both is required. Either service can be quickly deployed, along with a WAF Policy, in front of an existing public web application for testing. In production deployment scenarios, it is necessary to change the application configuration to allow only traffic from the new load balancer. This is covered in Chapter 9.

Permissions required for WAF deployment depend on the scope of the deployment. Creating and modifying a WAF Policy requires the following permissions:

- Microsoft.Network/frontDoorWebApplicationFirewallPolicies/write
- Microsoft.Network/ApplicationGatewayWebApplicationFirewallPolicies/write

Associating a WAF Policy with an application load balancing resource requires permissions to modify that resource, such as

- Microsoft.Network/frontDoors/write
- Microsoft.Network/applicationGateways/write

These permissions are part of the Network Contributor role, so you can use that role where appropriate. If changes to the application are necessary, such as restricting traffic to allow only the traffic coming from the WAF resource, permissions to modify the application are required. The application could be an Azure Web App, a web server on a VM, or something external to Azure.

Any Front Door or CDN endpoint can have a WAF Policy attached, but Application Gateway must be of the correct SKU tier. A WAF V2 tier is required to be able to use WAF Policy. Existing Application Gateways that are not of the correct type cannot be converted to WAF V2 and must be redeployed as the correct tier. Figure 5-2 shows the deployment options for Application Gateway.

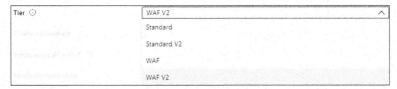

FIGURE 5-2   Azure Application Gateway tiers

Once the prerequisites are met, WAF Policies can be created and assigned to Application Gateways and Front Doors.

Policy creation

You create WAF Policies independently from the resources those policies will be assigned to. All WAF Policies are created using the same interface, but the wizard displays different options depending on which WAF type is selected. The initial deployment options for a new WAF Policy are shown in Figure 5-3.

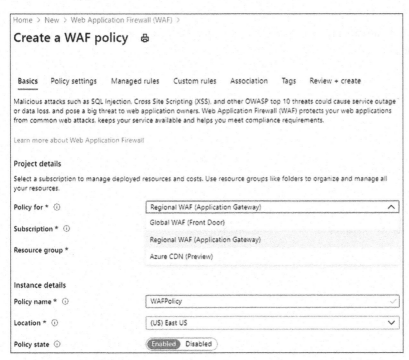

FIGURE 5-3   Azure WAF policy options

- **Policy For** This option specifies the WAF type. A policy created for one service cannot be applied to another.
- **Subscription** The subscription selected determines billing and permissions.
- **Resource Group** You can use a new or existing Resource Group.
- **Policy Name** The policy name must be unique to the Resource Group. Front Door and CDN Policies can only contain letters and numbers.
- **Location** (Application Gateway only) WAF Policies for Application Gateway must be assigned to a region and must exist in the same region as the Application Gateway it is associated with.
- **Policy State** To inspect traffic, even in detection mode, the policy must be in the Enabled state.

After the Basics tab has been filled in, the wizard presents different options based on the WAF type selected. These options are presented in the following sections.

Application Gateway WAF Policy creation

After navigating to Web Application Firewall policies (WAF) in the Azure portal, the process of creating a WAF Policy for Application Gateway is as follows:

1. Click **Add**.
2. On the **Basics** tab, **Select Application Gateways** in the **Policy for** field. Select a Subscription and Resource Group, and provide a unique name for the policy.
3. On the **Policy Settings** tab, you can change the following options, shown in Figure 5-4, if you choose:

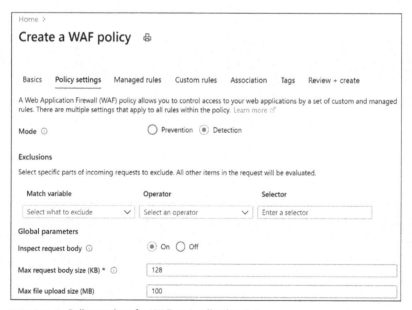

FIGURE 5-4 Policy settings for WAF on Application Gateway

- **Mode** The default is Detection mode, which only logs when WAF matches activity. Prevention mode is required to start blocking malicious traffic.

- **Exclusions** Meant for tuning, global exclusions instruct WAF to ignore entire fields when inspecting traffic. Tuning is covered in depth later in the chapter.

- **Inspect Request Body** This setting enables or disables inspection of the body of a web request. It is recommended that you leave this setting on to inspect every possible angle of attack.

- **Max Request Body Size** Requests larger than this limit are not inspected by WAF. Reducing this size can have a positive impact on performance but results in more requests passing through WAF without being inspected.

- **Max File Upload Size** WAF can limit the size of file uploads as an additional layer of security. The maximum size is 750MB.

4. On the Managed Rules tab, shown in Figure 5-5, assign one (or more) managed ruleset by checking the boxes in the drop-down menu:

FIGURE 5-5 Managed rule settings for WAF on Application Gateway

- **Managed Rule Set** Exactly one OWASP rule set must be enabled, and the Bot manager ruleset can optionally be enabled. More information about the rulesets is given later in the chapter in the "OWASP rules" section.

- **Enable/Disable Rules** By default, every rule is enabled. It is possible to disable individual rules at the time of policy creation, but it is recommended that you do this only if necessary as part of tuning, which is covered later in the chapter in the "OWASP rule tuning" section.

5. On the **Custom Rules** tab is the **Add Custom Rule option**, as shown in Figure 5-6, to add custom rules to the policy. During policy creation, custom rules are optional. All custom rule options are covered in depth later in the "Custom rules" section.

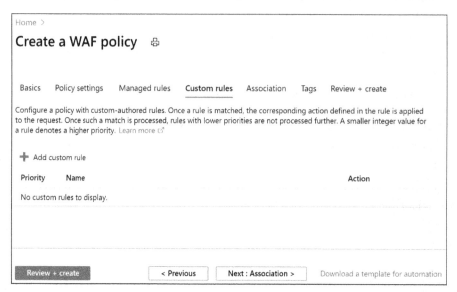

FIGURE 5-6 Custom rule settings for WAF on Application Gateway

6. On the **Association** tab, shown in Figure 5-7, choose where to assign the policy:

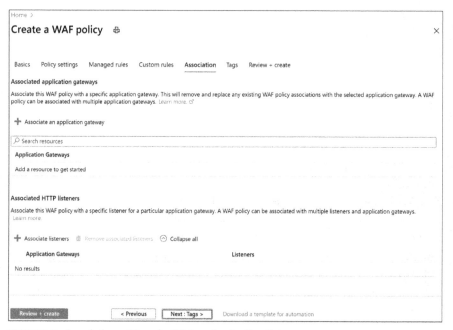

FIGURE 5-7 Association settings for WAF on Application Gateway

- **Associate an Application Gateway**   This option applies the newly created WAF Policy to the entire Application Gateway.
- **Associate HTTP Listeners**   This option applies the WAF Policy to specific listeners.

7. On the **Tags** tab, you can optionally assign tags to the resource.

8. When all options are finalized, review the information in the **Review + Create** tab. Now the WAF Policy can be created, including the association to the selected Application Gateways or listeners.

Front Door and CDN WAF Policy creation

Currently WAF policies cannot be shared among different attached services (Application Gateway, Front Door, and CDN). Because of this, it is necessary to create separate policies for use with each resource type.

The only difference between the policy options for the Front Door and CDN WAF policies is that CDN does not currently support the Bot Protection ruleset. After navigating to Web Application Firewall policies (WAF) in the Azure portal, use the following process to create a WAF Policy for Front Door:

1. Click **Add**.

2. On the **Basics** tab, Select Front Door in the **Policy for** field. Select a Subscription, Resource Group, and provide a unique name for the policy.

3. On the **Policy Settings** tab, shown in Figure 5-8, the following settings are optional to change from defaults:

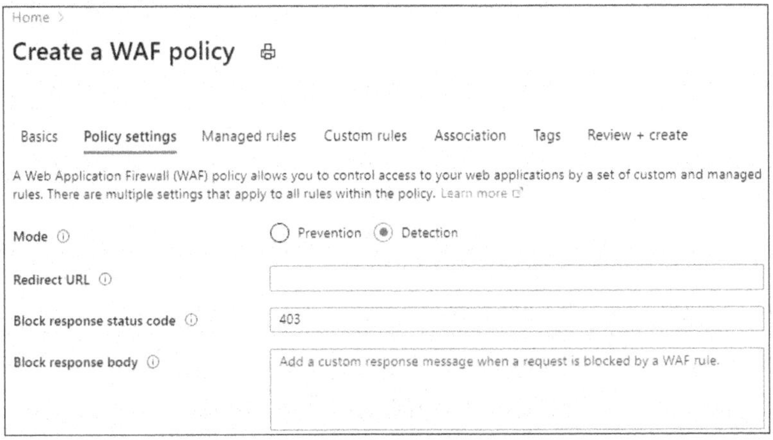

FIGURE 5-8   Policy settings for WAF on Front Door

- **Mode**   The default is Detection mode, which only logs when WAF matches activity. Prevention mode is required to start blocking malicious traffic.
- **Redirect URL**   WAF on Front Door offers the option to redirect requests (in addition to blocking or allowing). This URL is the destination for all redirect actions.

- **Block Response Status Code** By default, a standard 403 Forbidden HTTP status code is sent when requests are blocked. This gives the option to send a different status, including 200, 405, 406, or 429.

- **Block Response Body** This can be a string or HTML that is displayed when requests are blocked. By default, WAF on Front Door displays a simple block message that includes a logging ID for troubleshooting.

4. On the **Managed Rules** tab, select one or both managed rulesets as shown in Figure 5-9. Additional options are as follows:

FIGURE 5-9 Managed rule settings for WAF on Front Door

- **Managed Rule Set** One or both rulesets must be selected. The options are the DefaultRuleSet, which is focused on OWASP Top-10 detections, and the BotManagerRuleSet.

- **Enable/Disable Rules** By default, every rule is enabled, and it is possible to disable or change the action of individual rules at the time of policy creation. However, it is recommended that this be done only if necessary as part of tuning, which is covered later in the chapter.

5. On the **Custom Rules** tab, shown in Figure 5-10, optionally add custom rules to the policy by clicking **Add Custom Rule**. During policy creation, custom rules are optional. All custom rule options are covered in depth later in the chapter.

FIGURE 5-10   Custom rule settings for WAF on Front Door

6. On the **Association** tab, shown in Figure 5-11, associate the policy to a Front Door front end by clicking **Add Frontend Host**. This option applies the newly created WAF Policy to the selected Front Door front-end host.

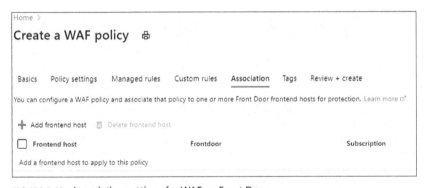

FIGURE 5-11   Association settings for WAF on Front Door

7. On the **Tags** tab, you can optionally assign tags to the resource.
8. After completing the previous steps, click **Review + Create** to check settings before the WAF Policy is created, including the association to the selected Front Doors.

Policy management

Because WAF Policies are created and managed independently from the resources they are associated to, there can be a many-to-many relationship among these resources. This means that one WAF Policy can be applied to several load balancing resources, or in the case of Application Gateway, many WAF Policies can be applied to several listeners on a single Application Gateway.

This potential complexity establishes the need to have a plan in place for managing policies at scale. Some common options include the following:

- **Customized Policies Per Association** This is the most secure option, wherein a new policy is created for every association, whether that is an entire Front Door or a single Application Gateway URI. The goal with this setup is to maintain maximum security protection from WAF by starting every deployment with the default policy configuration of all rules enabled, then tuning as needed for every association. Although this method incurs more management overhead, it has the advantages both of being as secure as possible and being certain that a change in a WAF Policy only affects a single association. One way to make this approach more efficient is to use a preconfigured ARM template as a starting point for customization.

- **Central Policies Associated Broadly** In this model, the goal is to reduce management overhead even if it is known to be at the expense of security. Policies are centralized as much as possible and associated to as many resources as possible. This method works very well when applications are similar, but when false positives occur and tuning is necessary, the downside becomes apparent. Any disabled rule or excluded field applies to everything the policy is associated to, which amounts to disabling inspection capabilities unnecessarily.

WAF rules and tuning

One goal of any security tool should be to provide the maximum protection possible while eliminating as many negative effects as possible to the function of the system being protected. For Azure WAF, this is accomplished by creating and enabling an effective set of rules and tuning those rules to meet the needs of the back-end application.

The managed rules available for Azure WAF include both OWASP rules and bot management rules. Both types are available by default when deploying a WAF Policy and are designed to protect against threats common to all customers and all applications.

The custom rules engine is designed to be open ended in order to be used as any administrator sees fit to protect against unique threats or to apply tuning to the most specific scope possible.

Policy deployment and tuning process

The deployment and tuning process for each WAF Policy follows the same path whether the policy is being deployed for the first time or newly associated. The broad process outline to follow when enabling WAF is the following:

- **Create Policy Or Select Existing** New or existing policies can be used as a starting point for a new association, and the subsequent parts of this outline can be used in either circumstance to ensure that the most secure and effective policy is in place.

- **Associate Policy In Detection Mode**   Detection mode ensures that all possible application paths and functions can be used during the testing period. It is recommended that all application functions be used during testing.

- **Observe Log Data**   In detection mode, WAF logs any rule matches, which indicates what traffic would have been blocked in prevention mode. During the testing phase, it is crucial that only legitimate traffic be sent to the web application to ensure that any rule matches encountered are false positives that can be tuned out. Tuning is done based on the rule matches in the log data. Logging is covered more comprehensively in Chapter 7, "Enabling Network Security log collection," and Chapter 8, "Security monitoring with Azure Sentinel, Security Center, and Network Watcher."

- **Tune Rulesets**   Tuning can take various forms, but it is always designed to eliminate false positives while keeping as much inspection active as possible.

- **Switch To Prevention Mode**   Once there is confidence that the vast majority of false positives have been eliminated, prevention mode should be enabled. At this point in the process, any rule matches will result in traffic being blocked, so it is important to have done sufficient testing before this stage.

- **Continuously Tune**   Once a stable state is reached, it is still necessary to monitor the WAF for false positives. These can be generated by legitimate traffic that was not represented in testing, new application features, or new rules. It is important to have some mechanism in place to detect potential issues before they affect users of the application.

The following sections give information to help with the tuning process, starting with developing a deep understanding of how each rule type works.

OWASP rules

The main ruleset of any WAF Policy is the OWASP ruleset, which is modeled and named after the Open Web Application Security Project, an organization that publishes guidance and tools geared toward protecting against the most common web application security vulnerabilities. These vulnerabilities are refreshed periodically and published on the OWASP website and are accessible at *https://aka.ms/AzNSBook/OWASP*.

To protect against many of the risks introduced by the OWASP Top 10, a group called SpiderLabs within the Trustwave security company developed a WAF engine and ruleset called the ModSec Core Rule Set, or CRS. The CRS is a recognized industry standard and the basis for the managed rulesets used by Azure WAF. More information follows in the chapter about the details of the WAF engine and rules.

Rule Logic

In WAF Policies for both Application Gateway and Front Door, the individual rules are each taken directly from the CRS. The major difference in how the two versions of the rulesets use the rules is that Application Gateway uses the entire CRS, whereas Front Door uses only a subset of the rules, pretuned to eliminate some that tend to cause an abundance of false positives.

For every rule included in a ruleset, there is a title and description that should convey the intent of the rule and what threats are being detected. To view these, visit Managed Rules in the WAF policy (for Application Gateway, each rule group must be expanded). There is also a search function to find rules of a particular type. The interface in a Front Door WAF policy is shown in Figure 5-12.

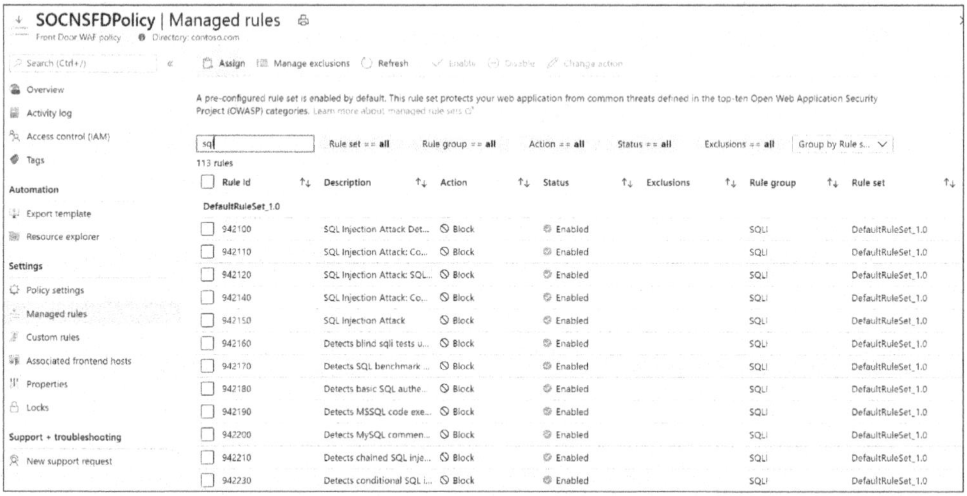

FIGURE 5-12 Rule details for WAF on Azure Front Door

To determine what each rule specifically matches, the rule ID must be taken and searched in the corresponding CRS repository:

- CRS 2.2.9 at *https://aka.ms/AzNSBook/CRS2*
- CRS 3.0 at *https://aka.ms/AzNSBook/CRS30*
- CRS 3.1 at *https://aka.ms/AzNSBook/CRS31*

The detailed rule breakdowns found in the CRS repositories are essential for understanding exactly what a rule is doing, especially when tuning becomes necessary. As an example, consider Rule ID 942230, a SQL Injection rule. The DefaultRuleSet in a WAF Policy for Front Door uses rules from the CRS 3.1. In the repository of the ruleset, rules are organized by group, each corresponding to the prefix of the Rule ID. To find Rule ID 942230, navigate to the file "REQUEST-942-APPLICATION-ATTACK-SQLI.conf" and search the page for the Rule ID as shown in Figure 5-13.

The most important part of the rule details is the regular expression that represents the matching logic of the rule. Many tools exist to analyze and test regular expressions, and there are some particularly effective ways to use the regular expressions found in the CRS repositories, including visualizing the matching logic using a tool called Regexper (*https://aka.ms/AzNSBook/Regex*). The interface is shown in Figure 5-14.

```
#
# -=[ SQL Injection Probings ]=-
#
# This is a group of three similar rules aiming to detect SQL injection probings.
#
# 942330 PL 1
# 942370 PL 2
# 942490 PL 3
# Regexp generated from util/regexp-assemble/regexp-942330.data using Regexp::Assemble.
# To rebuild the regexp:
#   cd util/regexp-assemble
#   ./regexp-assemble.pl regexp-942330.data
# Note that after assemble an outer bracket with an ignore case flag is added
# to the Regexp::Assemble output:
#   (?i:ASSEMBLE_OUTPUT)
#
SecRule REQUEST_COOKIES|!REQUEST_COOKIES:/__utm/|REQUEST_COOKIES_NAMES|ARGS_NAMES|ARGS|XML:/* "@rx (?i:(?:(?:(?:"[\"'`]\\\\]*?[^\"'`]+[\"'`]])+|(?:^[\"'`\\\\]*?[\d\"'`]+)+)\s*?(
    "id:942330,\
    phase:2,\
    block,\
    capture,\
    t:none,t:urlDecodeUni,\
    msg:'Detects classic SQL injection probings 1/3',\
    logdata:'Matched Data: %{TX.0} found within %{MATCHED_VAR_NAME}: %{MATCHED_VAR}',\
    tag:'application-multi',\
    tag:'language-multi',\
    tag:'platform-multi',\
    tag:'attack-sqli',\
    tag:'OWASP_CRS/WEB_ATTACK/SQL_INJECTION',\
    tag:'WASCTC/WASC-19',\
    tag:'OWASP_TOP_10/A1',\
    tag:'OWASP_AppSensor/CIE1',\
    tag:'PCI/6.5.2',\
    tag:'paranoia-level/2',\
    ver:'OWASP_CRS/3.1.1',\
    severity:'CRITICAL',\
    setvar:'tx.msg=%{rule.msg}',\
    setvar:'tx.sql_injection_score+=%{tx.critical_anomaly_score}',\
    setvar:'tx.anomaly_score_pl2+=%{tx.critical_anomaly_score}',\
    setvar:'tx.%{rule.id}-OWASP_CRS/WEB_ATTACK/SQLI-%{MATCHED_VAR_NAME}=%{tx.0}'"
```

FIGURE 5-13 Rule details in the CRS repository

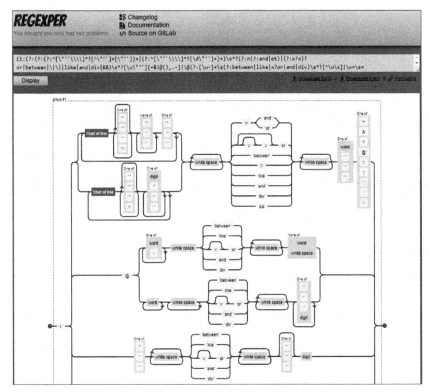

FIGURE 5-14 Regexper tool showing matching logic of a SQL injection rule

Other regular expression tools can be used to test the rule against strings, such as common requests to an application. This can be useful in tuning or developing custom rule logic based on the managed rules.

Anomaly scoring

An aspect of WAF detection logic that is only present in Azure WAF on Application Gateway is called anomaly scoring. Each rule is assigned an anomaly scoring level that assigns a numeric score to the rule. Each request inspected by Azure WAF has the potential to match one or multiple rules, and in anomaly scoring mode, the scores of each rule matched are added together to determine whether a block will occur. When in Prevention Mode, Azure WAF on Application Gateway blocks any request that has a cumulative anomaly score greater than or equal to 5.

In the 942330 SQL injection rule example, there is a line in the rule details that specifies the anomaly score of the rule:

```
"setvar:'tx.sql_injection_score=+%{tx.critical_anomaly_score}',\"
```

While the specification in the rule does not have a numeric value associated with it, the important piece to take note of is the word "critical." The possibilities for anomaly score are as follows:

- Critical: 5
- Error: 4
- Warning: 3
- Notice: 2

Given this score mapping, the SQL injection rule would have an anomaly score of 5 and would be blocked by WAF as long as it is in Prevention mode. By the same logic, a request that matches two rules, one with a Warning anomaly score and one with a Notice anomaly score, would also be blocked.

In contrast to the anomaly scoring behavior of Azure WAF on Application Gateway, Azure WAF on Front Door is binary in its logic; a match is blocked and a nonmatch is allowed. The reason WAF on Front Door operates in this way is due to the pretuning of the DefaultRuleSet. Rather than having all rules active, those that are less critical (lower anomaly score) are not present.

OWASP rule tuning

When false positives occur during testing of the OWASP managed rules, it is a straightforward process to eliminate them. It is always best to identify rule matches in the logs while the WAF is in Detection mode than to discover false positives after WAF has gone live in Prevention mode because traffic was blocked.

If Diagnostic Logs have been enabled and are being written to Log Analytics (more on this in Chapter 7), any rule match is logged. Note that the blocking logic is different between Azure WAF on Application Gateway versus Front Door, so there are different considerations to make when determining whether a request would be blocked.

For WAF on Front Door, if a rule match is logged, it would have been blocked. For Application Gateway, the individual rule matches and their anomaly scores must be taken into consideration. Techniques for analyzing log data are covered in depth in Chapter 8.

When a rule is found to be causing false positives, it can be modified for tuning. In the case of Application Gateway, the options for modifying each rule are either Enable or Disable, as shown in Figure 5-15. A disabled rule completely stops the WAF engine from inspecting traffic with the rule, so logging of rule matches also is disabled. Another consideration to make before disabling a rule is that the change affects any Application Gateway or Listener associated with the policy.

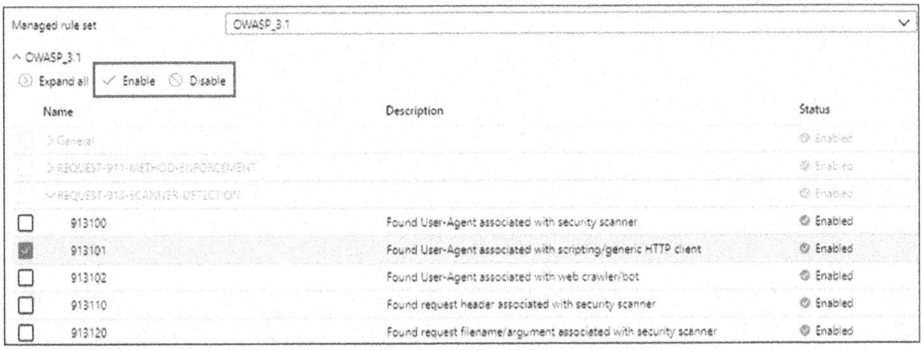

FIGURE 5-15 Managed rule tuning on WAF for Application Gateway

With Azure WAF on Front Door, there are different options for each rule, including Allow, Block, Log, or Redirect (see Figure 5-16). The Log option is useful if blocking is not necessary, but visibility into rule matches is still valuable. Just as with WAF Policies for Application Gateway, any change in rule actions affects all associations of the policy.

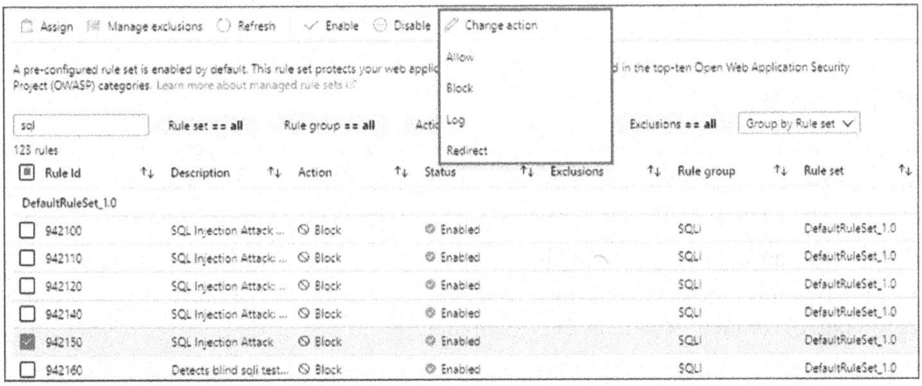

FIGURE 5-16 Managed rule tuning on WAF for Front Door

Bot management rules

Azure WAF uses IP reputation to determine whether traffic is associated to known bots. The reputation information is sourced from an internal Microsoft service that aggregates threat intelligence from various internal and external sources. The application of this data to WAF inspection differs slightly between the Application Gateway and Front Door implementations of WAF.

The Bot Management ruleset for WAF on Front Door includes several rules, categorized as good, bad, or unknown bots. The default actions differ for each category. Bad bots are blocked, good bots are allowed, and unknown bots are logged, as shown in Figure 5-17. These default rule actions can be changed to Allow, Block, Log, or Redirect.

Microsoft_BotManagerRuleSet_1.0					
Bot100100	Malicious bots detected by threat intelligence	Block	Enabled	BadBots	Microsoft_BotManagerRuleSet_1.0
Bot100200	Malicious bots that have falsified their identity	Block	Enabled	BadBots	Microsoft_BotManagerRuleSet_1.0
Bot200100	Search engine crawlers	Allow	Enabled	GoodBots	Microsoft_BotManagerRuleSet_1.0
Bot200200	Unverified search engine crawlers	Log	Enabled	GoodBots	Microsoft_BotManagerRuleSet_1.0
Bot300100	Unspecified identity	Log	Enabled	UnknownBots	Microsoft_BotManagerRuleSet_1.0
Bot300200	Tools and frameworks for web crawling and attacks	Log	Enabled	UnknownBots	Microsoft_BotManagerRuleSet_1.0
Bot300300	General purpose HTTP clients and SDKs	Log	Enabled	UnknownBots	Microsoft_BotManagerRuleSet_1.0
Bot300400	Service agents	Log	Enabled	UnknownBots	Microsoft_BotManagerRuleSet_1.0
Bot300500	Site health monitoring services	Log	Enabled	UnknownBots	Microsoft_BotManagerRuleSet_1.0
Bot300600	Unknown bots detected by threat intelligence	Log	Enabled	UnknownBots	Microsoft_BotManagerRuleSet_1.0
Bot300700	Other bots	Log	Enabled	UnknownBots	Microsoft_BotManagerRuleSet_1.0

FIGURE 5-17 Bot management rules on WAF for Front Door

On Application Gateway, the Bot Management ruleset is simpler, detecting only malicious bots and offering the options to enable or disable the rule. The Application Gateway Bot ruleset is shown in Figure 5-18.

Microsoft_BotManagerRuleSet_0.1		
Expand all Enable Disable		
Name	**Description**	**Status**
KnownBadBots		Enabled
1	Malicious Bots	Enabled

FIGURE 5-18 Bot management rules on WAF for Application Gateway

Custom rules

The custom rules engine in Azure WAF is able to perform various functions outside the scope of what the managed rulesets can do. Custom rules are evaluated before managed rules, so some traffic can be filtered out before even needing to be processed by the managed rulesets.

Custom rules can also evaluate multiple conditions, giving them the ability to evaluate requests for a complex set of criteria. The possibilities for custom rules are vast, so here are just a few examples of common scenarios for custom rules:

- **IP allow or block list**   Rules can be constructed to match based on an array of IP addresses. An example of this rule logic is shown in Figure 5-19.

- **Rate limiting**   WAF on Azure Front Door is able to rate-limit traffic by detecting repeated requests from the same source and applying a limit to that traffic. This must be combined with at least one condition, such as a string or address match. An example of a rate limiting rule is shown in Figure 5-20.

FIGURE 5-19 Custom WAF rule to allow only certain IP addresses and ranges

FIGURE 5-20 Custom WAF rule to rate-limit requests to specific paths

- **Geographical restrictions** Geo-location rules can be used to either allow or deny traffic from certain regions. An example of a geographic allow list is shown in Figure 5-21.

FIGURE 5-21 Custom WAF rule to allow only certain geo-locations

- **Multicondition matches** Any of the preceding logic can be combined into multipart conditional matches. When adding conditions to a rule, the operator is always "AND," meaning that all conditions must be satisfied to result in a match.

Exclusions

Excluding fields from WAF inspection can be an effective method for eliminating false positives. If it is determined that one or multiple rules are matching content in particular fields, those fields can be excluded from inspection. This is an alternative to disabling the rule.

WAF on Front Door is able to exclude fields from inspection from the entire ruleset, rule groups, or individual rules. Configuration of exclusions for this WAF type is done as part of the managed rules interface. Options for rule exclusions on a Front Door WAF policy are shown in Figure 5-22.

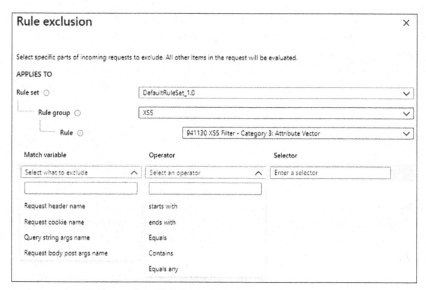

FIGURE 5-22   Exclusion options for WAF on Front Door

WAF on Application Gateway operates in a different way, as exclusions are assigned only to the entire policy. You configure exclusions in the Policy Settings blade. This is shown in Figure 5-23.

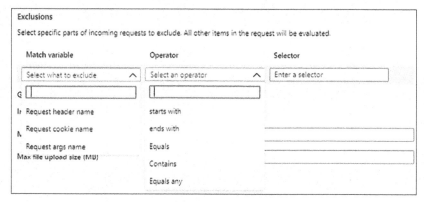

FIGURE 5-23   Exclusion options for WAF on Application Gateway

It is important to consider the fact that excluding fields from inspection has the potential to open an application up to vulnerabilities.

Policy assignment for tuning

The various tuning methods covered in this chapter involve making changes to WAF Policies. A very important factor to consider when making these changes is where the policies in question are associated. Specifically for WAF on Application Gateway, policies can be associated to entire Application Gateways, listeners, or individual URIs.

When evaluating the potential impact of a change to a policy, remember that any tuning adjustment has the effect of reducing the inspection capabilities of WAF. This being the case, it can be a good decision to assign a tuned policy only to what the tuning has a positive effect on. For example, if it is necessary to exclude a field from inspection or disable a rule that otherwise has security value, it may be best to apply the tuned policy to only the URI or listener that is seeing false positives.

Summary

This chapter has detailed the need to secure applications as part of a comprehensive network security strategy in Azure. Writing secure application code is a fundamental part of this strategy, but Azure WAF should be added as a supplementary layer of security. In addition to providing defense in depth by preventing common exploits, WAF can add additional security controls via custom rules or bot mitigation rulesets.

A key takeaway from this chapter is that WAF deployment is not complete after creating and associating a WAF policy. The tuning process is essential to making sure that false positives are minimized, and that log data is well understood by the teams that use it.

Using the information presented in this chapter, you should now be able to apply an additional layer of exploit detection and prevention to your web applications in Azure, whether they are delivered using Application Gateway or Front Door.

## Chapter 6

Mitigating DDoS attacks

D istributed denial-of-service (DDoS) attacks continue to grow in both intensity and prevalence. The goal of a DDoS attack is to disrupt the availability of a service to its intended consumers. The distributed nature of these attacks (distinct to regular denial-of-service attacks) means that the attacks originate from multiple remote sources. The mechanisms used by attackers to carry out this disruption are both inexpensive and effective, which enables a continuing upward trend in attack volume and frequency.

Any service that is accessible over the internet, including those hosted in Azure, are potential targets for DDoS attacks. Many companies host their primary websites in Azure, and an interruption in availability could cost thousands or even millions of dollars over the course of an attack. For these reasons, it is important to make preparations to mitigate the risk of a DDoS attack by designing application infrastructure for resiliency, using the attack mitigation tools available in Azure, and ensuring that response procedures are in place.

This chapter primarily focuses on Azure DDoS Protection, which exists in two forms—Basic and Standard. The chapter discusses the capabilities of both versions of the service, as well as the important differences between them. There are some DDoS attacks that fall outside the scope of the primary DDoS Protection mechanism in Azure; to account for those, the chapter covers some Azure WAF features.

> **TIP**   See the Microsoft Digital Defense Report for more analysis on recent DDoS and other attack trends at *https://aka.ms/AzNSBook/DDR*.

How Azure DDoS Protection Works

Azure DDoS Protection is divided into two tiers in terms of cost (Basic, or platform protection, is free, whereas Standard is subject to Azure consumption costs), but both services use the same mechanism to mitigate attacks. The exact process that the mechanism uses to mitigate attacks is covered in the next section.

It is important to understand exactly which types of attacks that Azure DDoS Protection is designed to mitigate. The primary OSI layers involved in traffic bound for Azure are Layers 3, 4, and 7, which are the network, transport, and application layers. Azure DDoS Protection focuses on the attacks targeting Layers 3 and 4:

- **Layer 3**   Network attacks, also called volumetric attacks, seek to inhibit the ability of traffic to reach the destination. This is done by sending as much traffic as possible to the target to cause enough network congestion that legitimate requests are unable to reach their intended destination. These attacks are usually aided by some sort of reflection or amplification, as seen in attacks like the Memcached attacks of 2018.

> **TIP**   For more details, see the MITRE ATT&CK description at *https://aka.ms/AzNSBook/NetworkDDoS.*

- **Layer 4**   Transport layer attacks, or protocol attacks, seek to exploit inherent attributes or limitations in the protocols used to transport traffic. These attacks do not necessarily saturate the network connection to the destination, as in network attacks. Instead, certain traffic types are sent to cause a protocol-specific bottleneck. In the example of a SYN Flood, the TCP handshake process is started over and over by sending SYN packets from multiple sources. This is intended to exhaust the connections that can be handled by each back-end server.

> **TIP**   For more details, see the MITRE ATT&CK description at *https://aka.ms/AzNSBook/TransportDDoS.*

Azure DDoS Protection is designed to detect and mitigate both network and transport layer attacks against Azure resources. The goal of the service is to maintain availability of any Azure resource during one of these types of attacks. This is done by dropping any malicious traffic and allowing legitimate traffic, the process of which is detailed in the next section.

The mitigation pipeline

The actual technology used to observe traffic and determine its legitimacy is done by proprietary technology referred to as the mitigation pipeline. Although we can't publicly share many of the inner workings of this pipeline, we can give an overview of how the system works and how traffic ends up there.

An important concept to cover is the fact that DDoS Protection works at the level of the public IP address in Azure. An external, or publicly routable, IP is always the entry point for traffic from the public internet to Azure networks. This IP address may be an actual Azure resource (public IP address) that is part of a customer subscription and able to be managed via the Azure portal, or it could be Microsoft owned and managed, possibly part of a multitenant PaaS service like Azure Front Door. The options differ for which Azure DDoS Protection tier is available depending on whether the IP is managed by the customer or Microsoft, but the concept of DDoS Protection applying to this IP address remains the same.

For any public IP address in Azure, traffic inbound from the internet fluctuates within some observable range. To detect a potential DDoS attack against a particular IP address, Azure DDoS Protection sets a threshold, measured in packets per second, at some level above the observed "normal" traffic levels for an IP address. This threshold represents the point at which an increase in traffic could be considered a potential DDoS attack. The threshold is actually three separate metrics and is set differently depending on which tier of Azure DDoS Protection is being used. The logic behind setting thresholds is covered in the next section, and viewing thresholds using Azure Monitor Metrics is discussed later in the chapter in the "Metrics" section.

When traffic volume surpasses a threshold, rather than being routed within Azure's internal network directly to the intended destination, traffic is rerouted to pass through the mitigation pipeline first. The purpose of the pipeline is to observe traffic and drop malicious traffic while still allowing legitimate traffic. The pipeline only looks at traffic properties of Layers 3 and 4, so does not go as far as terminating TLS to inspect application content. Even at the network and transport layers, a number of inspection and mitigation techniques are able to be used effectively to block malicious traffic. By inspecting attributes such as packet size, IP options, TCP flags, and other elements, traffic can be dropped outright or rate limited based on high volume sources. Figure 6-1 shows the path of traffic as it enters the Azure network bound for a protected public IP address.

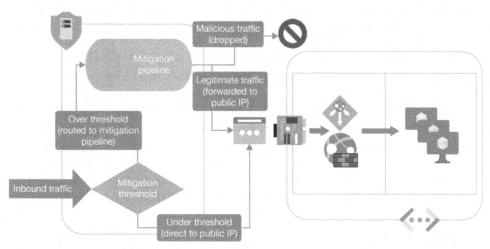

FIGURE 6-1   Azure DDoS Protection traffic flow diagram

The mitigation period, or the span of time between the change in routing to the mitigation pipeline and when the route is returned to normal, lasts until the observed traffic volume has dropped back below the threshold. The effect of the potential attack and the resulting mitigation should not be felt by the resource being attacked as long as the application has been designed to handle the initial traffic spike. Even in the event that the mitigation is a false-positive, such as in the case of a retail website receiving an abrupt increase in traffic during a holiday sale, legitimate traffic is all sent through the pipeline without being dropped for any reason, and the application functions as normal.

DDoS Protection Basic versus Standard

The technology used in the mitigation pipeline is the same across Azure regardless of the tier of service being used, but there are important differences between the free platform-level protection, also called Basic, and the paid service, called Standard.

A helpful way to understand the difference between tiers is that platform protection is primarily designed to protect Azure itself, whereas Azure DDoS Protection Standard is meant to protect individual assets in customer virtual networks. This is not to say that platform protection does not protect customer-managed assets; there is a great deal of protection provided by the platform protection, but it is not as fine-tuned to individual workloads as Standard, and it does not provide as much visibility and extra protection.

Some of the important additional capabilities of Azure DDoS Protection Standard, which are shown in Figure 6-2, include the following:

- **Application-based mitigation thresholds** This is the most fundamental difference between Basic and Standard and is a primary reason why customers choose to enable the paid version of the service. Thresholds were discussed in the previous section as the determining factor for diverting traffic to the mitigation pipeline, and how these thresholds are set is the primary differentiator between Basic and Standard. With platform protection, or Basic, the thresholds for each public IP address are set based on an aggregated average of all traffic to the region. Since this level of protection is primarily designed to protect the Azure infrastructure, these thresholds tend to be high. In practice, this could mean that a small to moderately sized attack below these thresholds could affect an individual Azure resource without triggering mitigation because the attack is not large enough to register as a threat to the Azure region. With Azure DDoS Protection Standard, thresholds are set dynamically based on learned traffic volumes to each protected IP address. The threshold automatically adjusts to changing traffic patterns over time, so the threshold remains a reasonable level above normally observed traffic. Having a precisely set threshold is advantageous because any spike in traffic is sure to be quickly routed to the mitigation pipeline, increasing the speed and overall effectiveness of the mitigation process.

- **Cost protection** When a DDoS attack occurs, there is a period of time between when traffic levels spike and when the malicious portion of traffic is dropped by the mitigation pipeline, usually 60 to 90 seconds. While waiting for routes to be announced to divert traffic to the mitigation pipeline, all traffic is sent to whatever resources are downstream from the public IP address receiving traffic. If the resources behind that IP automatically scale out in response to the increased traffic volume, such as in the case of an Application Gateway v2 with a Virtual Machine Scale Set as its back-end pool, these autoscale events would normally incur extra costs. With Azure DDoS Protection Standard applied, any costs incurred because of scale-out during a verified attack are credited back to the customer.

- **Metrics** You can use Azure Monitor to view any DDoS Protection metrics associated with public IP address resources. These metrics include the mitigation thresholds, which are viewable any time for each protected IP address, and several different attack mitigation metrics, which are generated only during mitigation.

- **Logs** When Azure DDoS Protection Standard is enabled, you can enable three categories of diagnostic logs (DDoSProtectionNotifications, DDoSMitigationFlowLogs, and DDoSMitigationReports) on public IP address resources. The process for enabling these logs is discussed in Chapter 7, "Enabling network security log collection," and best practices for using these logs as part of a security monitoring strategy are covered in Chapter 8, "Security monitoring with Azure Sentinel, Security Center, and Network Watcher."

- **DDoS rapid response support** Although the expectation is that a DDoS attack mitigated by Azure DDoS Protection Standard results in minimal or no downtime (assuming a well-architected application or service), there is a benefit to having high-priority support. Azure support engineers are available to assist during any mitigation event if for any reason customization of the function of the mitigation pipeline is necessary.

Feature	Azure Platform DDoS Protection (Basic)	Azure DDoS Protection Standard
Active traffic monitoring and detection	◆	◆
Automatic attack mitigation	◆	◆
Automatically tuned mitigation thresholds per public IP address		◆
Cost protection		◆
Metrics and Diagnostic logs		◆
Rapid response support		◆

FIGURE 6-2 Comparison table for Azure DDoS Protection Standard versus Platform (Basic)

The decision of whether to opt into the paid service or to be content with the protection provided by platform protection comes down to risk tolerance. For many companies, the increased effectiveness of the adaptive threshold tuning, combined with the financial assurance of cost protection, is enough to justify the extra cost. The extra data generated by Azure DDoS Protection Standard, along with the promise of high-priority support, is sometimes a requirement for security-focused teams.

There is a limit to which resources can be protected by Azure DDoS Protection Standard, which is a very important concept to understand. The Standard tier can be applied only to public IP address resources that are associated with customer virtual networks. As a general rule, when searching for resources in the Azure portal of the public IP address type, the list of IP addresses and the resources attached to them represent the full list that is eligible for Azure DDoS Protection Standard.

The most common resource types that are considered high priority to protect include Application Gateways, Azure Firewalls, Load Balancers, VPN Gateways, and Network Virtual Appliances. Standard virtual machine IP addresses can be covered by DDoS protection, and many customers do so, but depending on the workload running on the machine and the services exposed to inbound traffic, they may or may not be considered a target of value.

DDoS Protection Options for PaaS Services

Notably missing from the list of resources that can be protected by Azure DDoS Protection Standard are non-VNet-associated PaaS services, such as Azure Storage, SQL, CDN, and Front Door. Also outside the scope of Standard are nonstandard-VNet services such as API Management (APIM), App Service Environment (ASE), and Virtual WAN.

In the case of PaaS services, there are options for DDoS Protection. If the Standard tier is required, then the service must be put behind a VNet resource such as an Azure Web App as a back-end pool member of an Application Gateway. Similar scenarios can be accomplished using Azure Firewall to pass traffic to a Private Link–enabled Azure Storage instance. These scenarios make the most sense when other features of the intermediary service are also required, such as Azure WAF on Application Gateway or Threat Intelligence on Azure Firewall.

Unless there is a compelling reason to complicate the architecture, platform protection or Basic can usually provide more than adequate protection for PaaS resources. The thresholds for the IP addresses used by Azure to serve these resources are set in accordance with the capability of the service to handle increases in traffic volume. Because PaaS services are cloud native and designed for scale, they are able to handle traffic spikes regardless of whether the threshold is set higher than one may be set for a VNet service. For this reason, many of the benefits of Azure DDoS Protection Standard become less important for resources of this type.

Enabling Azure DDoS Protection Standard

This section goes through the steps necessary to enable Azure DDoS Protection Standard, as well as best practices to get the most out of the service. The process of enabling and configuring Standard can be summarized in the following steps:

1. Create a DDoS Protection plan
2. Associate virtual networks to the DDoS Protection plan
3. Enable diagnostic logs and metrics with Azure Monitor

Although it is the Public IP Address resource type that is being protected by the plan, the VNet is the resource type that is associated to the plan. Public IP addresses are always associated with a network interface resource, and network interfaces are always associated with a virtual network. To protect public IP addresses, the VNet where the Network Interface is associated must be attached to a DDoS Protection Plan.

Within minutes after making the association between VNet and DDoS Protection Plan, the associated public IP addresses are protected from attack. It is important to finish the configuration by enabling the logging and metrics available because this is one of the valuable aspects of upgrading to Azure DDoS Protection Standard.

Create a DDoS Protection plan

A single DDoS Protection plan can be used to cover every eligible resource in a tenant, so multiple Azure subscriptions and VNets can be protected by a central plan. There are circumstances where multiple plans are desired, such as for multiple tenants or to separate resources for chargeback. Under most circumstances, though, a single DDoS Protection plan is the recommended approach.

The cost associated with Azure DDoS Protection Standard is based on the number of plans and the number of public IP address resources associated with each plan. The first 100 IP addresses are covered by the monthly fee for the service, and each IP address after the first 100 incurs an additional cost proportional to the cost of the first 100 (monthly fee divided by 100). At the time of this writing, the monthly cost is $3,000 USD, so a plan with 75 IP addresses associated would cost $3,000 per month, and a plan with 250 IP addresses associated would cost $7,500 per month. Keep these costs in mind when deciding whether to use just one plan or multiple.

Creating a DDoS Protection plan is as simple as navigating to the **DDoS Protection Plans** blade in the Azure portal. This is pictured in Figure 6-3.

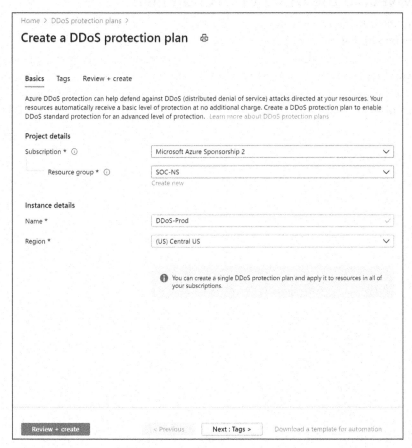

FIGURE 6-3 Creating a DDoS Protection Plan

The few options available to configure during the plan creation process are as follows:

- **Subscription** Since the plan can be associated with VNets in any subscription, selecting a particular subscription here does not have any effect on which resources it can apply to. The primary importance of this option is cost management. The costs for the plan are associated to the subscription selected in this option. Commonly, the subscription used here is a centrally managed one for security or networking.

- **Resource Group** Like the selection of subscription, the choice for Resource Group has no effect on the function of the plan, but permissions may be a factor to consider. You can use a new or existing Resource Group.

- **Name** The name must be unique within the Resource Group.

- **Region** The location has no effect on the function of the plan.

After a DDoS Protection plan has been created, it neither provides any protection nor incurs any cost until VNets containing public IP addresses are associated.

Associate VNets to the DDoS Protection plan

Once a plan exists, there are two ways to attach virtual networks to the plan via the Azure portal, depending on whether the VNet is new or existing. For new VNets, there is an option to attach to a DDoS Protection plan built in to the VNet creation wizard. After completing the **Basics** and **IP Addresses** tabs, you can use the **Security** tab to attach a DDoS Protection Plan, deploy an Azure Firewall, or deploy a Bastion Host. The VNet creation method of attaching DDoS Protection is pictured in Figure 6-4.

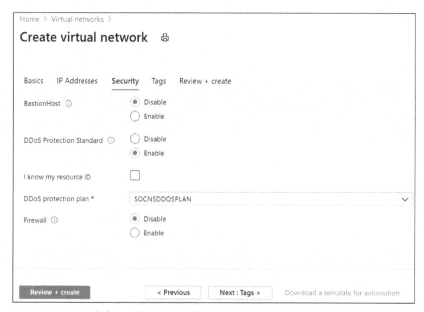

FIGURE 6-4 Associating a DDoS Protection plan when creating a VNet

When attaching existing VNets to a plan, you can complete the process using the **DDoS Protection** blade of the virtual network resource, which is pictured in Figure 6-5. This process is likely easier to perform at scale using methods such as PowerShell, Az CLI, or Azure Policy. See *https://aka.ms/AzNSBook/DDoSPolicy* for an example of how to accomplish this with Azure Policy.

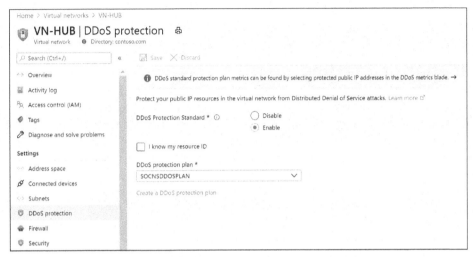

FIGURE 6-5   Associating a DDoS Protection plan on an existing VNet

After you complete the steps of creating the DDoS Protection plan and associating VNets, protection of the IP addresses associated with the protected VNets become active quickly. The final steps in the process include verifying which resources are protected and enabling data collection.

Finishing deployment

Once you have attached VNet resources to a DDoS Protection plan, you can view which public IP address resources are protected by navigating to the **Protected Resources** blade of the **DDoS Protection** Plan resource. This view is shown in Figure 6-6.

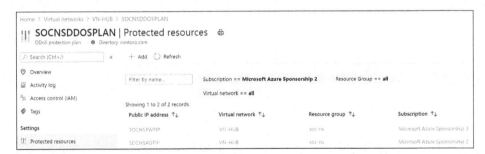

FIGURE 6-6   The Protected Resources Blade of the DDoS Protection Plan Resource

One of the most common drivers for enabling Azure DDoS Protection Standard is to collect the relevant data for security teams to analyze. For this reason, enabling Standard without configuring logging and metrics cannot be considered a complete deployment. Even if not every public IP address is intended to be protected by a plan, it is a best practice to enable logging and metrics on every public IP address resource. Logs are generated only during mitigation events, so no extraneous data will be generated.

You can find full details on enabling and using logs and metrics in Chapters 7 and 8.

Validation and testing

Following complete deployment of Azure DDoS Protection Standard, you may want to test the service and its efficacy in mitigating attacks against Azure hosted resources. The goal of tests can be to record the result of an attack against a protected resource (whether that service remains available) and generate logs for the purpose of validating alerts, dashboards, and response procedures.

Metrics

Once you've enabled metrics on protected IP addresses, you can view them either in the Metrics blade of the DDoS Protection Plan resource or via Azure Monitor. The first metrics to take note of are the thresholds for mitigation. The importance of thresholds has been stated several times in this chapter, and they can be seen in real time using metrics.

To view thresholds, use the following process:

1. Navigate to the **Metrics** blade of **Azure Monitor**.

2. Upon entering the **Metrics** blade, select a scope by specifying a resource to display metrics about. Select a subscription and filter resource types to public IP addresses, as shown in Figure 6-7.

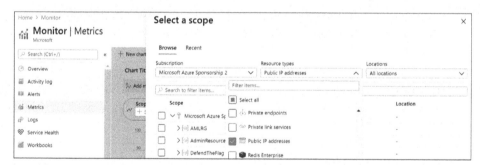

FIGURE 6-7 Choosing a scope to add a resource to a metric chart in Azure Monitor

3. Expand **Resource Group**, check the box of the IP address to view, and click **Apply**.

4. Click **Add Metric** and select **Inbound SYN Packets To Trigger DDoS Mitigation** from the Metric drop-down menu, as shown in Figure 6-8. Aggregation can be kept to the default, **Max**.

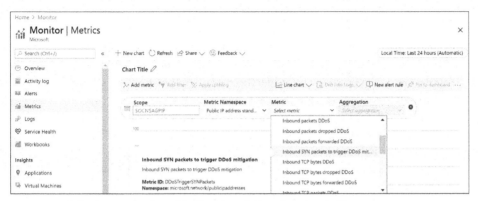

FIGURE 6-8 Selecting metrics for public IP address SYN packets threshold

5. Repeat the Add Metric process for both **Inbound TCP Packets To Trigger DDoS Mitigation** and **Inbound UDP Packets To Trigger DDoS Mitigation**. The resulting chart is pictured in Figure 6-9.

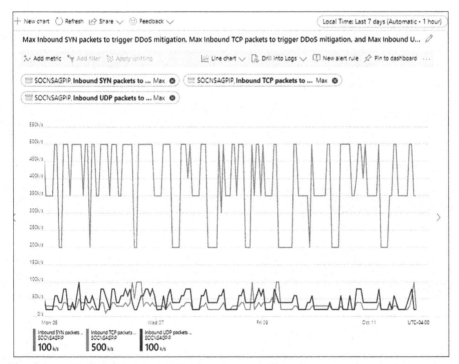

FIGURE 6-9 All three DDoS thresholds plotted on one chart

Once all three threshold metrics have been added, they can all be visualized on the same chart and time can be sliced as necessary. These values fluctuate over time as the service learns traffic patterns. The numbers represented in Figure 6-9 are in packets per second, and this represents the traffic rate at which mitigation will be triggered, re-routing traffic through the mitigation pipeline.

Another important metric is a very basic one that describes whether a Public IP Address resource is under active mitigation at any point in time. This metric is called Under DDoS Attack Or Not, and the metric can be added to a separate chart using the same process described previously. This metric is plotted on the chart in Figure 6-10.

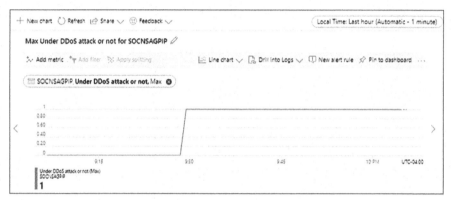

FIGURE 6-10 The Under Attack Or Not Metric

During an active mitigation event, several other metrics are recorded, which can be useful to analyze what is happening. The full list of available metrics, including those already discussed is

- Byte Count
- Data Path Availability
- Inbound Bytes DDoS
- Inbound Bytes Dropped DDoS
- Inbound Bytes Forwarded DDoS
- Inbound Packets DDoS
- Inbound Packets Dropped DDoS
- Inbound Packets Forwarded DDoS
- Inbound SYN Packets To Trigger DDoS Mitigation
- Inbound TCP Bytes DDoS
- Inbound TCP Bytes Dropped DDoS
- Inbound TCP Bytes Forwarded DDoS
- Inbound TCP Packets DDoS
- Inbound TCP Packets Dropped DDoS

- Inbound TCP Packets Forwarded DDoS
- Inbound TCP Packets To Trigger DDoS Mitigation
- Inbound UDP Bytes DDoS
- Inbound UDP Bytes Dropped DDoS
- Inbound UDP Bytes Forwarded DDoS
- Inbound UDP Packets DDoS
- Inbound UDP Packets Dropped DDoS
- Inbound UDP Packets Forwarded DDoS
- Inbound UDP Packets To Trigger DDoS Mitigation
- Packet Count
- SYN Count
- Under DDoS Attack Or Not

These additional metrics can be assembled into a number of useful charts. One example is shown in Figure 6-11.

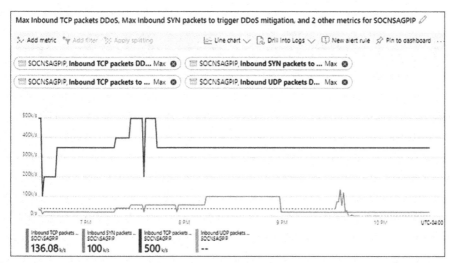

FIGURE 6-11 Inbound packet metrics plotted alongside thresholds

Validation with BreakingPoint Cloud

Microsoft has partnered with Ixia to provide a great tool for testing the effectiveness of Azure DDoS Protection Standard and generating attack data. BreakingPoint Cloud is a service that can be used to perform a variety of test attacks against Azure resources at configurable traffic volumes.

The service is available to purchase for regular ongoing use, which is suitable for organizations that carry out regular testing of their security controls and response plans. There is also a free trial available, which allows for 5GB of data usage. The data available for the free trial is sufficient in many cases to trigger a mitigation, but it depends on the thresholds that are in place. If a threshold is below the Test Size as specified in the test configuration in Breaking-Point, the test triggers a DDoS mitigation. See the previous section to find the threshold values for an IP address.

Once an account is created and logged into the BreakingPoint portal, the Azure subscription(s) where the target public IP addresses reside must be authorized to test against. This can be done by selecting Azure Subscriptions from the Settings (gear) drop-down menu and entering a subscription ID. This prompts the user to allow BreakingPoint to read the list of public IP address resources in the subscription. As long as it can be determined that the test is being conducted against authorized resources, the tests will pass validation and be allowed to continue. The subscription validation interface is shown in Figure 6-12.

> **TIP** Although it's meant for testing, attacks from BreakingPoint are very real in the sense that they send large traffic volumes to the target, which can cause disruption to the availability of the service. Use appropriate notification and change control procedures before testing against any resources.

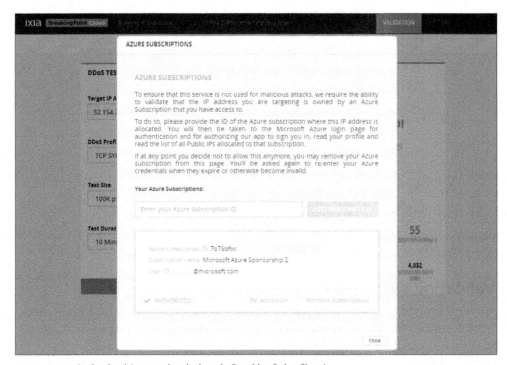

FIGURE 6-12 Authorized Azure subscriptions in BreakingPoint Cloud

There are only a few options that need to be configured before initiating an attack, which include the following:

- **Target IP Address** This is the destination of the attack traffic. Before testing, it is recommended that you verify that the public IP address resource is listed as a protected resource and that logs and metrics have been configured.

- **Port Number** This is the destination port of the attack traffic. Using an open port, such as 80 or 443 for a web application, is recommended that you simulate a real attack and test the resiliency of the service behind the IP address.

- **DDoS Profile** This setting specifies the attack type that will be used for the test. The options include

  - DNS Flood
  - NTPv2 Flood
  - SSDP Flood
  - TCP SYN Flood
  - UDP 64B Flood
  - UDP 128B Flood
  - UDP 256B Flood
  - UDP 512B Flood
  - UDP 1024B Flood
  - UDP 1514B Flood
  - UDP Fragmentation
  - UDP Memcached

- **Size** Attack size, measured in both packets per second and Mbps/Tbps, varies in options available, depending on the attack profile. This setting should reflect a packets-per-second value that is higher than the threshold for the protocol.

- **Duration** Attacks can last from 10 to 30 minutes.

Figure 6-13 shows a BreakingPoint test configuration fully configured and ready to start.

Once a test is started, BreakingPoint validates that the IP address is owned by the account that authorized the subscription; then traffic will begin. Progress can be monitored while the test is ongoing, as shown in Figure 6-14.

During and after the test, data is generated by Azure DDoS Protection Standard, and analysis can begin. Detection and mitigation of the attack takes about 60 seconds to begin, and logs follow shortly after.

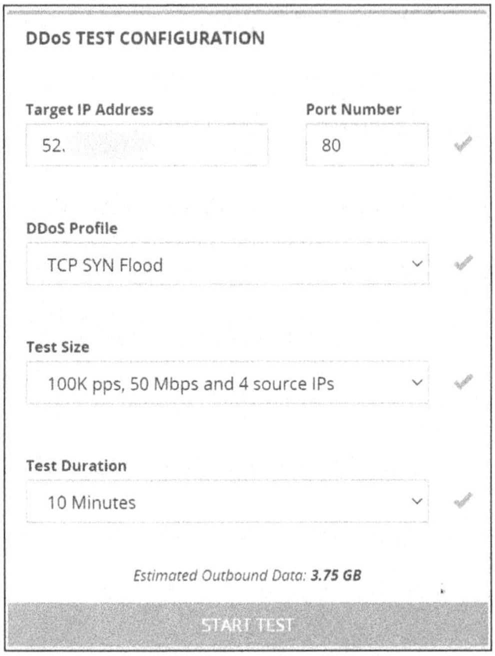

FIGURE 6-13 BreakingPoint Cloud test configuration options

FIGURE 6-14 A BreakingPoint Cloud test in progress

Log samples

When diagnostic logs are enabled for public IP address resources, there are three available categories: DDoSProtectionNotifications, DDoSMitigationFlowLogs, and DDoSMitigationReports. For reference, samples of each type follow.

DDoS protection notifications (DDoSProtectionNotifications) are the first log to be generated during a mitigation event. These logs are generated only when mitigation starts or stops, and they include basic information about the mitigation activity, such as the IP address being attacked and the reason for mitigation. A sample is shown in Figure 6-15.

TenantId	8ecf8077
TimeGenerated [UTC]	2020-09-23T06:54:55.571Z
ResourceId	/SUBSCRIPTIONS/7B76BFBC /RESOURCEGROUPS/SOC-NS/PROVIDERS/MICROSOFT.NETWORK/PUBLICIPADDRESSES/SOCNSFWPIP
Category	DDoSProtectionNotifications
ResourceGroup	SOC-NS
SubscriptionId	7b76bfbc-cb1e-4df1-
ResourceProvider	MICROSOFT.NETWORK
Resource	SOCNSFWPIP
ResourceType	PUBLICIPADDRESSES
OperationName	DDoSProtectionNotifications
Message	[MITIGATION STARTED] Start DDoS mitigation for 52. Inbound SYN traffic exceeds DDoS protection threshold: 100000 SYN packets per second
type_s	MitigationStarted
SourceSystem	Azure
publicIpAddress_s	52.
Type	AzureDiagnostics
_ResourceId	/subscriptions/7b76bfbc /resourcegroups/soc-ns/providers/microsoft.network/publicipaddresses/socnsfwpip

FIGURE 6-15 The details of a DDoS protection notification log

DDoS mitigation flow logs (DDoSMitigationFlowLogs) are the most abundant of the DDoS logs generated. Every request that traverses the mitigation pipeline is logged to this category, which includes properties such as source IP address, port, and whether the request was forwarded to the destination or dropped. A sample is shown in Figure 6-16.

TenantId	8ecf8077
TimeGenerated [UTC]	2020-09-23T01:15:19.903Z
ResourceId	/SUBSCRIPTIONS/7B76BFBC /RESOURCEGROUPS/SOC-NS/PROVIDERS/MICROSOFT.NETWORK/PUBLICIPADDRESSES/SOCNSAGPIP
Category	DDoSMitigationFlowLogs
ResourceGroup	SOC-NS
SubscriptionId	7b76bfbc-cb1e-4df1-
ResourceProvider	MICROSOFT.NETWORK
Resource	SOCNSAGPIP
ResourceType	PUBLICIPADDRESSES
OperationName	DDoSMitigationFlowLogs
Message	Packet was forwarded to service
SourceSystem	Azure
sourcePublicIpAddress_s	40.
sourcePort_s	443
destPublicIpAddress_s	52.
destPort_s	3075
protocol_s	tcp
Type	AzureDiagnostics
_ResourceId	/subscriptions/7b76bfbc /resourcegroups/soc-ns/providers/microsoft.network/publicipaddresses/socnsagpip

FIGURE 6-16 The details of a DDoS mitigation flow log

DDoS mitigation reports (DDoSMitigationReports) are sent at five-minute intervals during the course of mitigation, then a final report is sent at the end of mitigation. These logs contain aggregated statistics that have been taken from the flow log data and enriched. Summaries of traffic types and locations of origin are included, along with other useful summary data. A sample is shown in Figure 6-17.

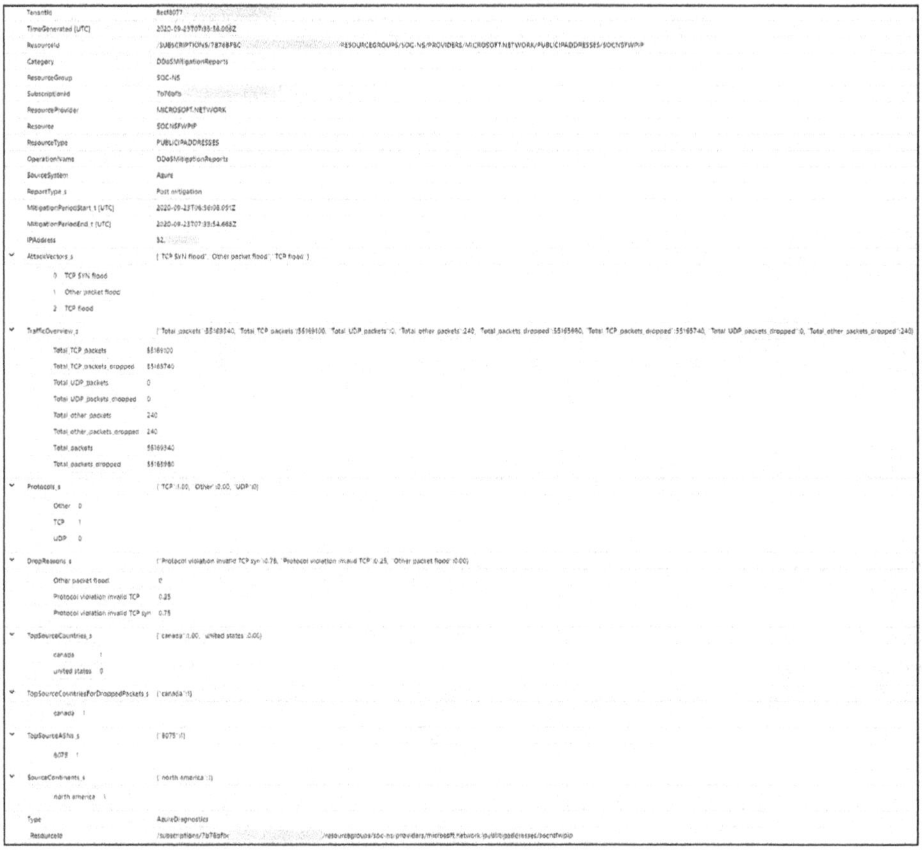

FIGURE 6-17 The details of a DDoS mitigation report log

Enabling and using these logs with security tools is covered in Chapters 7 and 8.

Application resiliency

During testing and validation, it is important to validate that mitigation starts at the appropriate threshold and that data is generated to record blocked traffic, but it is equally important to ensure that the vital services being protected remain available. The point of DDoS Protection, after all, is to protect against threats to the availability of Azure resources.

In the very beginning of the attack, as the spike in volume is recognized and routing to the mitigation pipeline is announced, there is a period of time roughly 60 seconds in duration during which attack traffic will be forwarded to the IP address it is intended for. In this amount of time, there could be negative impact to the resource behind the IP address if the application is not designed appropriately. It is highly recommended that you use autoscaling services that can adapt to increased load, such as Virtual Machine Scale Sets or Application Gateway v2. If services like these are not in use, services have a greatly reduced likelihood of becoming available again, even after mitigation starts.

> **TIP** For more information on building applications for scale, see *https://aka.ms/AzNSBook/AutoScaling.*

Summary

This chapter should convey the necessity of protecting Azure resources against DDoS attacks, as well as the processes to follow to enable Azure DDoS Protection Standard. While deploying the service is a very quick process, there are other steps involved that should not be skipped. It is important to ensure that all valuable resources are associated to the plan and that all logging is enabled to support security operations.

## Chapter 7

Enabling Network Security log collection

Azure provides various levels of logging and auditing from Azure Activity Logs to resource logs. Activity logs provide operational logs of each resource (which is also known as the data plane) and can be exported to various destinations. Resource logs are also known as diagnostic logs. The three destinations are Azure Monitor Log Analytics for cloud monitoring and analysis, Azure Event Hubs for forwarding outside of Azure, and Azure storage for archiving. Organizations can configure one or more destinations—for example, if they are requirements for long-term archiving (storage) and active monitoring (Log Analytics). A diagnostic setting is created to configure resource logs.

It is important for organizations to collect these logs for active analysis or investigation of security incidents. For example, if a VM is compromised, the SOC may want to look at the Azure Firewall traffic to and from that machine to look for a unique IP address. These may indicate IP addresses to block or further monitor to see if other resources may be compromised. The logs could also be used to create additional alert rules in services like Azure Sentinel for further detections above and beyond what the service provides. Because all the logs discussed in this chapter are security related, it is recommended that they are stored in the same Log Analytics workspace. Azure Sentinel can then be enabled on that workspace.

In this chapter, we cover enabling Azure resource logs for Firewall, DDoS, WAF, and Bastion. We also discuss using Network Watcher to configure NSG Flow Logs and Traffic Analytics. Azure Monitor Log Analytics is the common destination for all data generated. We also discuss how to broadly apply the configurations using Azure Policy. Chapter 8, "Security monitoring with Azure Sentinel, Security Center, and Network Watcher," covers more in depth on how to use the data in various ways.

> **TIP** This chapter does not concentrate on understanding Azure Monitor Log Analytics. For more information on Azure Monitor Log Analytics, *see https://aka.ms/AzNSBook/LogA.*

Network traffic logging

Logging network traffic can be useful for a variety of reasons. Alerts can be generated when Indication of Compromises (IoCs) are seen in the traffic, auditors want to ensure that you have a handle on what network traffic is traversing your network, security analysts need to use traffic as part of investigations, or system administrators need to use the traffic for troubleshooting issues like application performance or possible DoS (denial of service) attacks.

Aggregating syslog traffic from your network devices or collecting ETW (Event Tracing for Windows) network traffic from your servers into a searchable database like Kusto or Splunk allows for all of the described scenarios. The data from devices should be normalized from each of the different systems into fields such as time (UTC), IP, the associated device that owns that IP address, the body of the message, and a raw data field that contains the original data that was received. This makes it possible to create easy-to-use queries to facilitate alerting, auditing, and investigation of the traffic.

For investigations, an integrated device management/asset management database that relates device and OS to IP is critical. This allows easy pivoting/spidering when observing the data to see what other devices and IP addresses are involved in the investigation and what vulnerabilities may lie in those devices. For an investigator, this is critical to discovering what assets are involved in an investigation.

Ken Hollis, Security Analyst, Microsoft Security Response Center

David Fosth, Principal Security PM Manager, Microsoft Security Response Center

Azure Firewall

Azure Firewall provides logging for Metrics, Application Rules, DNS Proxy, Network Rules, and Threat Intelligence. The diagnostic settings are configured on the Firewall resource, even when using Azure Firewall Manager. Use the following steps to create the diagnostic setting:

1. Open the **Azure portal** and sign in as a user who has Monitoring Contributor privileges to the Azure Firewall resource. The user also needs Log Analytics Contributor or Log Analytics Reader to access to the workspace to be used as the destination.
2. In the search pane, type **Firewalls** and click the **Firewalls** icon when it appears.
3. Select the **Firewall** resource to configure.
4. In the left pane, click **Diagnostic Settings**, as shown in Figure 7-1.

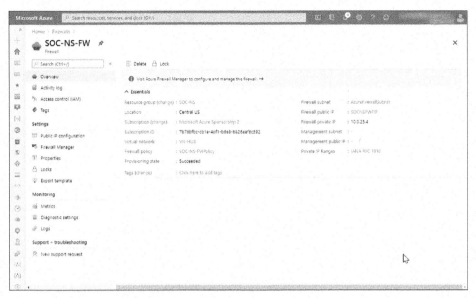

FIGURE 7-1 The Azure Firewall Resource blade

5. Click **Add Diagnostic Setting**, as shown in Figure 7-2.

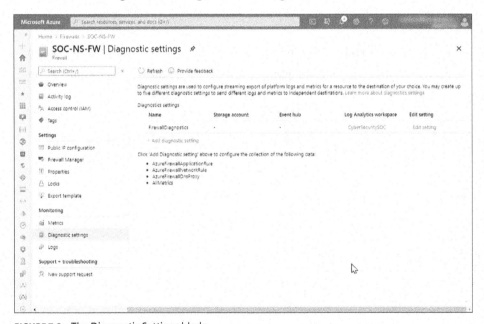

FIGURE 7-2 The Diagnostic Settings blade

6. Check the logs and metrics to be collected. Check **Send To Log Analytics**. Select the subscription and workspace from the drop-down menus. Click **Save**. Figure 7-3 shows an example configuration.

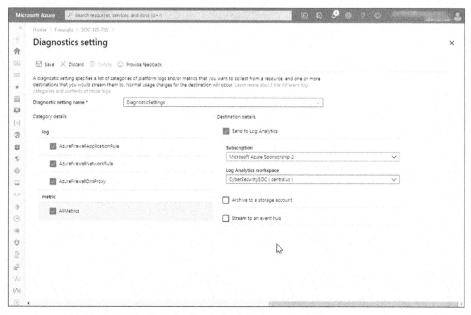

FIGURE 7-3 The Diagnostic Settings Configuration blade

Once the setting is enabled, it may take a few minutes for logs to begin flowing. To view the logs, use the following steps:

1. Open the **Azure portal** and sign in as a user who has Log Analytics Reader permissions.

2. In the search pane, type **Log Analytics** and click the **Log Analytics Workspaces** icon when it appears.

3. Select the workspace that **you** configured in the previous steps, as shown in Figure 7-4.

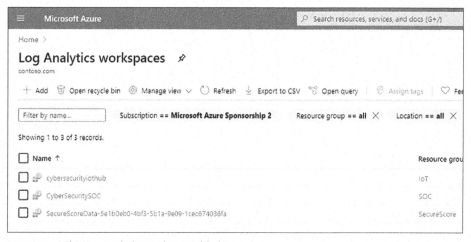

FIGURE 7-4 The Log Analytics workspaces blade

4. Click the **Logs** blade from the left menu, as shown in Figure 7-5.

FIGURE 7-5   The Log Analytics blade

5. If you have not visited the Logs blade before, you get the **Example Queries** pop-up window shown in Figure 7-6. You can see in the figure there are example queries for Firewall. If this pop-up window doesn't appear, you can click **Example Queries** on the Logs blade to reach it.

TIP   For more information on Example Queries, see *https://aka.ms/AzNSBook/ExampleQueries.*

6. Click **Run** on the **Application Rule Log** data as shown in Figure 7-7.

7. Figure 7-8 shows the example query was loaded and run.

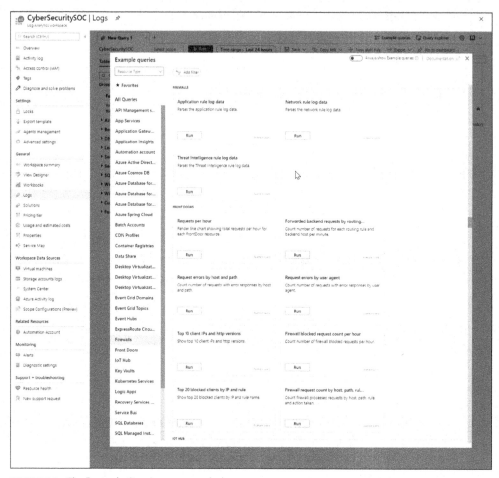

FIGURE 7-6 The Example Queries pop-up window

FIGURE 7-7 Azure Firewall example queries

FIGURE 7-8 The Logs blade with an example query loaded and run

For Azure Firewall there are four categories in Azure Diagnostics:

- AzureFirewallNetworkRule
- AzureFirewallDnsProxy
- AzureFirewallApplicationRule
- AzureFirewallThreatIntelLog

Chapter 8 covers using the different logs for monitoring, reporting, and analytics in depth.

Web Application Firewall

WAF policy is a central resource applied to Application Gateway or Front Door resources. This means Diagnostics settings are configured on the App Gateway or Front Door resource. CDN WAF is a bit different. Diagnostic settings are configured directly on this resource. Use the following steps to create the diagnostic setting:

1. Open the **Azure portal** and sign in as a user who has Monitoring Contributor privileges to the Application Gateway resource. The user also needs Log Analytics Contributor or Log Analytics Reader privileges to access to the workspace to be used as the destination.

2. In the search pane, type **Application Gateway** and click the Application Gateway icon when it appears.

3. Select the **Application Gateway** resource to configure for log collection.

4. In the left pane, click **Diagnostic Settings**, as shown in Figure 7-9.

5. Click **Add Diagnostic Setting**, as shown in Figure 7-10.

FIGURE 7-9 The Azure Web Application Gateway blade

FIGURE 7-10 Add diagnostic setting

6. Check the logs and metrics to be collected. Check **Send To Log Analytics**. Select the subscription and workspace from the drop-down menus. Click **Save**. Figure 7-11 shows an example configuration. You can see the log types are different for WAF.

FIGURE 7-11 The Diagnostic Settings Configuration blade

Once the setting is enabled, it may take a few minutes for logs to begin flowing. To view the logs, use the following steps:

1. Open the **Azure portal** and sign in as a user who has Log Analytics Reader permissions.

2. In the search pane, type **Log Analytics** and click the Log Analytics workspaces icon when it appears.

3. Select the workspace that you configured in the previous steps.

4. Click **Logs**.

5. Enter the following query and click **Run**:

```
AzureDiagnostics
| where Category == "ApplicationGatewayFirewallLog"
```

The WAF on Application Gateway logging schema is documented at *https://aka.ms/ AzNSBook/AppGWWAFLogs*.

The previous sets of steps are the same for Azure Front Door except the category is Front-doorWebApplicationFirewallLog. The Front Door WAF logging schema is documented at *https://aka.ms/AzNSBook/FDWAFLogs*.

For CDN WAF, you configure the Diagnostic setting on the WAF policy, as shown in Figure 7-12.

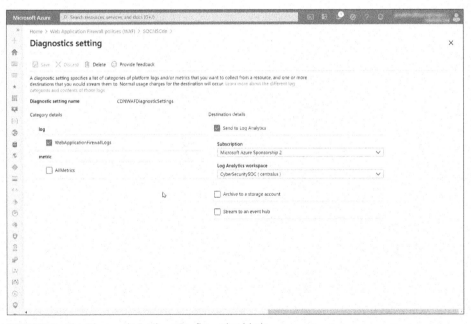

FIGURE 7-12 The Diagnostic Settings Configuration blade

Azure DDoS Protection Standard

Azure DDoS Protection Standard is also a central resource. This means Diagnostics settings are configured on the public IP resources that are protected by Azure DDoS. Use the following steps to create the diagnostic setting:

1. Open the **Azure portal** and sign in as a user who has Monitoring Contributor privileges. The user also needs Log Analytics Contributor or Log Analytics Reader privileges to access to the workspace to be used as the destination.

2. In the search pane, type **Monitor** and click the **Monitor icon** when it appears.

3. In the left pane, click **Diagnostic Settings**, as shown in Figure 7-13.

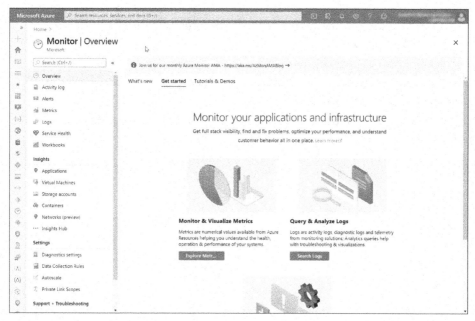

FIGURE 7-13   The Azure Monitor blade

4. Filter to the **Resource Group** and **Resource Type**. Click the resource as shown from the list in Figure 7-14.

5. Click **Add Diagnostic Setting**.

6. Check the logs and metrics to be collected. Check **Send To Log Analytics**. Select the subscription and workspace from the drop-down menus. Click **Save**. Figure 7-15 shows an example configuration.

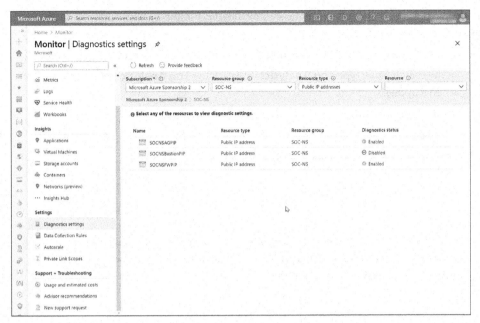

FIGURE 7-14 The Diagnostic Settings blade

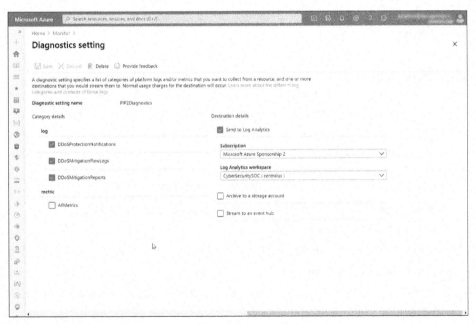

FIGURE 7-15 The Diagnostic Settings Configuration blade

Once the setting is enabled, it may take a few minutes for logs to begin flowing. To view the logs, use the following steps:

1. Open the **Azure portal** and sign in as a user who has Log Analytics Reader privileges.

2. In the search pane, type **Log Analytics** and click th**e Log Analytics Workspaces icon** when it appears.

3. Select the workspace that you configured in the previous steps.

4. Click **Logs**.

5. Enter the following query and click **Run**:

```
AzureDiagnostics
| where Category == "DDoSProtectionNotifications"
```

> **Note** If a DDoS attack has not occurred, there may not be any logs available yet. An organization can validate DDoS protection to generate some logs. See https://aka.ms/AzNSBook/ValidateDDOS

For Azure DDoS Protection there are three categories in Azure Diagnostics:

- DDoSProtectionNotifications
- DDoSMitigationFlowLogs
- DDoSMitigationReports

Azure Bastion

The diagnostic settings configuration is configured on the Bastion resource. Use the following steps to create the diagnostic setting:

1. Open the **Azure portal** and sign in as a user who has Monitoring Contributor privileges. The user also needs Log Analytics Contributor or Log Analytics Reader privileges to access to the workspace to be used as the destination.

2. In the search pane, type **Bastion** and click the Bastion icon when it appears.

3. Select the **Bastion** resource to configure.

4. In the left pane, click **Diagnostic Settings**, as shown in Figure 7-16.

5. Click Add **Diagnostic Setting**.

6. Check the logs and metrics to be collected. Check **Send To Log Analytics**. Select the subscription and workspace from the drop-down menus. Click **Save**. An example configuration is shown in Figure 7-17.

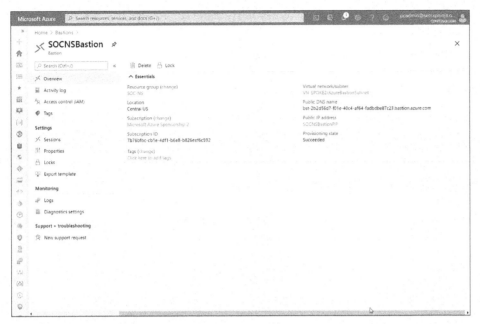

FIGURE 7-16 The Azure Bastion blade

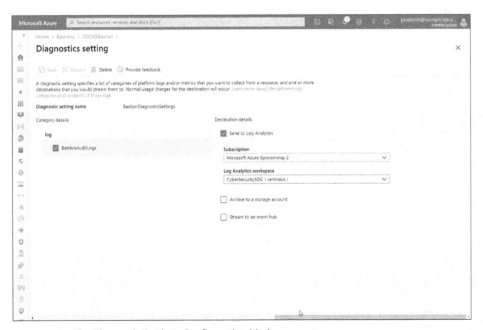

FIGURE 7-17 The Diagnostic Settings Configuration blade

Once the setting is enabled, it may take a few minutes for logs to begin flowing. To view the logs, use the following steps:

1. Open the **Azure portal** and sign in as a user who has Log Analytics Reader privileges.

2. In the search pane, type **Log Analytics** and click the **Log Analytics Workspaces icon** when it appears.

3. Select the workspace that you configured in the previous steps.

4. Click **Logs**.

5. Enter the following query and click **Run**:

```
AzureDiagnostics
| where Category == "BastionAuditLogs"
```

Network Security Groups

NSGs (Network Security Groups) provide diagnostic logs for events and rule counters. Events are which NSG rules are applied to virtual machines, and rule counters provide information counting the number of connections that match a rule for a resource. These can be useful information. Like previous steps covered earlier, you enable the diagnostic settings on the NSG resource. See Figure 7-18.

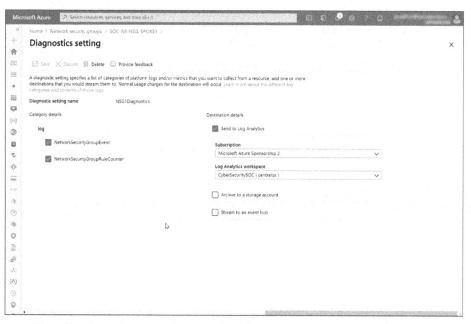

FIGURE 7-18   The Diagnostic Settings Configuration blade

From a security perspective, these logs are not particularly useful because they don't contain the source IP address. The logs can also be expensive to collect due to the high quantity. NSG provides the ability to log flows that pass through the NSG resource, known as flow logs. To collect and analyze flow logs, you must use the Traffic Analytics service. Traffic Analytics is part of Network Watcher and can allow for the visualizing activity, understanding traffic patterns, and finding configuration issues.

Traffic Analytics processes the raw NSG flow logs and reduces the logs by aggregating common flows. The aggregation looks at source IP, destination IP, port, and protocol. Traffic Analytics can then write the aggregated logs to Log Analytics. Use the following steps to enable Traffic Analytics:

1. Open the **Azure portal** and sign in as a user who has Monitoring Contributor privileges. The user also needs Log Analytics Contributor or Log Analytics Reader privileges to access to the workspace to be used as the destination.

2. In the search pane, type **Network Watcher** and click the **Network Watcher icon** when it appears.

3. In the left pane, click **NSG Flow Logs**, as shown in Figure 7-19.

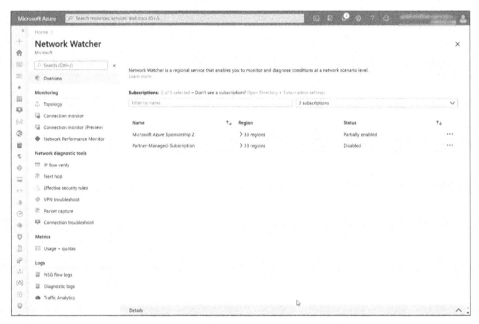

FIGURE 7-19 The Azure Network Watcher blade

4. Select an **NSG Resource** to configure, as shown in Figure 7-20.

5. Click **On**.

6. Select **Version 2**.

7. Configure a **Storage Account**.

8. Click **On** for **Traffic Analytics**.

9. Select **Every 10 mins** for processing.

10. Configure a **Log Analytics** workspace.

11. Click **Save**. Figure 7-21 shows an example configuration.

FIGURE 7-20 The Diagnostic Settings blade

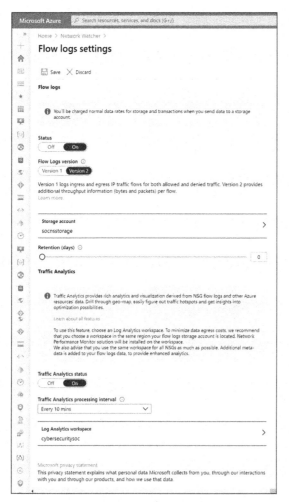

FIGURE 7-21 The Diagnostic Settings Configuration blade

Once the setting is enabled it may take 20 to 30 minutes for logs to begin flowing. To view the logs, use the following steps:

1. Open the **Azure portal** and sign in as a user who has Log Analytics Reader privileges.

2. In the search pane, type **Log Analytics** and click the **Log Analytics Workspaces icon** when it appears.

3. Select the workspace that you configured in the previous steps.

4. Click **Logs**.

5. Enter the following query and click **Run**:

```
AzureNetworkAnalytics_CL
```

Traffic Analytics provides several views and slices of the data that are useful. For more information, see *https://aka.ms/AzNSBook/TrafficAnalytics*. Figure 7-22 shows the Traffic Analytics overview blade. There are several reports you can click to view the data in more depth.

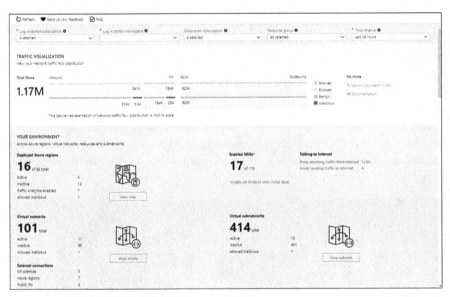

FIGURE 7-22 The Traffic Analytics blade

Diagnostic settings at scale

It is not ideal to manage Diagnostic Settings for each of the network security resources that get deployed. You can manage it if there are only one or two, but in larger organizations, it's not reasonable to do so. Additionally, applying central policies to ensure logging is enabled on network security resources ensures no logs are missed, which will not be known until an attack occurs and the logs are needed.

Figure 7-23 shows there are some built-in policies for auditing or deploying diagnostic resources. An organization can use these to centrally deploy the configuration across resources.

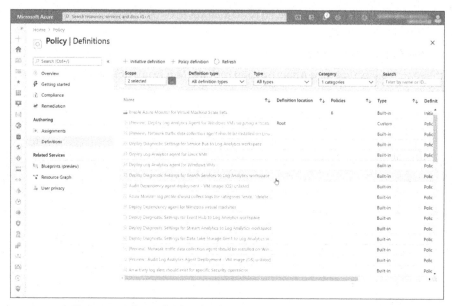

FIGURE 7-23 The Azure Policy Definitions blade

If a built-in policy does not exist for a particular resource, there is a great community contribution from Jim Britt at *https://aka.ms/AzNSBook/PolicyScript*. The script can enumerate resources in the Azure environment, check whether they support diagnostic settings, and create a sample policy to be used to configure the environment. The output is ARM templates that can be deployed to Azure Policy. Figure 7-24 shows the output of policy samples for network security resources.

FIGURE 7-24 Output from the community script to create policy definitions

Summary

In this chapter, we reviewed how to enable the various diagnostics logs for each Azure Network Security service. Chapter 8 goes further into how and why you would use these logs to detect and investigate security incidents. A key takeaway is that each service has different types of logs that are available. It's up to you to enable the logs that you need in your environment to detect and respond to possible incidents.

Chapter 8

Security monitoring with Azure Sentinel, Security Center, and Network Watcher

Written by Mike Kassis

The previous chapter explains how to turn on logging and consolidate logs into a few areas. It also touched on some of the querying capabilities across these logs. This chapter explores how to start working with those logs. In some cases, we will have out-of-the-box (OOTB) alerting capabilities and investigation tools, which are extremely useful for handling 80% of your monitoring use cases. For the other 20%, we can build custom queries, playbooks, workbooks, and alerts. Knowing what is available and when to use a specific approach are critical to operationalizing your use of the Azure network security product stack.

First, we look at Security Center and how we can see recommendations and alerts. Next, we move into Azure Sentinel, Microsoft's cloud-native Security Information and Event Monitoring (SIEM) solution, where we discuss connectors, workbooks, playbooks, and incident management. Finally, we wrap up with Network Watcher's traffic testing tools and network topology mapping.

We touch a lot of topics in this chapter, but at the end you should have a good understanding of what exists, where the components are located, and when to use each solution. You should then build on these foundational concepts and take your learning further by visiting the formal documentation for each area.

Security Center

Security Center, previously named Azure Security Center (ASC), is an Azure-hosted security solution aimed at centralizing cloud posture management and providing advanced threat detection and protection both inside and outside of Azure. Previously, Security Center had a free tier focused on cloud security posture management (CSPM) and a standard tier focused on cloud workload protection (CWP) for your hybrid cloud resources. Recently, these tiers were dissolved, and you now have Security Center, which is wholly focused on CSPM and Azure Defender, which is the new cloud workload protection platform (CWPP). In this section, we touch on network security capabilities of Security Center as well as Azure Defender.

Security Center provides recommendations to show which of your networking resources are currently being monitored versus which have not had monitoring enabled. For those resources that are being monitored, it also shows which resources are in a healthy state versus an unhealthy state.

Security policies

In Security Center, security policies, shown in Figure 8-1, dictate what recommendations you see, and every tenant has a standard policy created and applied as soon as you enable Security Center. By following these recommendations, you are helping to ensure a strong security posture for your organization. In the realm of network security, this means keeping an eye on network configurations as well as ensuring Azure DDoS, Azure Firewall, and Azure App Gateway WAF are enabled where appropriate.

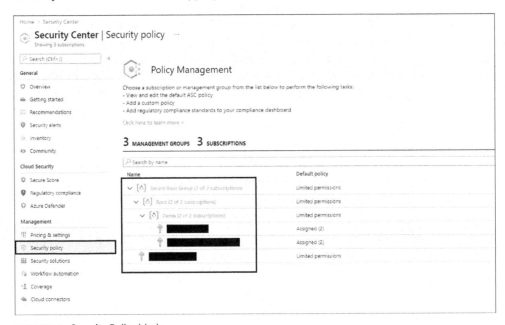

FIGURE 8-1 Security Policy blade

To find what rules are enabled in a specific policy, you can select **Security Policy** and choose a management group or subscription as shown in Figure 8-2.

There are three sections that make up an overall policy. Two of them are enabled OOTB: the Security Center Default Policy and Industry & Regulatory Standards. The final option, Custom Initiatives, is where you can add optional recommendations that may not be in the default policy.

Security policy ...
CESECDEP - Internal

Security policy on: ▇▇▇▇▇▇▇▇

Policies enabled on this subscription

Security Center default policy

This is the default policy for Azure Security Center recommendations which is enabled by default on your subscriptions.

Assignment	Assigned On	Audit policies	Deny policies	Disable policies	Exempted policies	
ASC Default (subscript...	Subscription	181	1	7	0	...

Industry & regulatory standards

Your custom initiatives

Custom initiative policies which you have created which are available in the **Recommendations** page. To add another custom initiative policy, click **Add a custom initiative.**

Tiander-initiative	test	Delete
Yanivsh -Show audit results from Windows VMs that have Google Chrome installed		Delete
Diagnostic Checks		Delete
Woodgrove Benchmark		Delete

Add a custom initiative

FIGURE 8-2 Security Policy for a selected subscription

At the time of writing, both Azure Firewall and Azure DDoS have default recommendations available in Security Center and Azure App Gateway (WAF) has available custom policies that can be added to the custom recommendations section. Azure Firewall is the newest addition to the lineup of recommendations and will show you which virtual networks do not have Azure Firewall enabled. As for Azure DDoS, you will see the following recommendation: Azure DDoS Protection Standard Should Be Enabled On Your Applications. In Figure 8-3, this recommendation is under the Protect Applications Against DDoS Attacks section, assuming you have at least one applicable resource.

∨ Protect applications against DDoS attacks	+ **1%** (1 point)	1 of 10 resources	▇▇▇▇▇▇▇
Azure DDoS Protection Standard should be enabled		1 of 9 virtual networks	▇▇▇▇▇▇▇
Azure Policy Add-on for Kubernetes should be install... ⊚ Completed		None	▇▇▇▇▇▇▇
Container CPU and memory limits should be enforced ⊚ Completed		None	▇▇▇▇▇▇▇
Web Application Firewall (WAF) should be enabled f... Preview		1 of 1 Application Gate...	▇▇▇▇▇▇▇
Web Application Firewall (WAF) should ... ⊚ Completed Preview		None	▇▇▇▇▇▇▇

FIGURE 8-3 Recommendations in Security Center

For App Gateway WAF, there are currently no built-in recommendations. However, you can still add WAF definitions to a custom initiative. Navigate to the **Add Custom Initiatives** section and search for "waf." You should see the following recommendations (also shown in Figure 8-4):

- WAF should be enabled for Azure Front Door Service.
- WAF should use the specified mode for Application Gateway.
- WAF should use the specified mode for Azure Front Door Service.
- WAF should be enabled for Application Gateway.

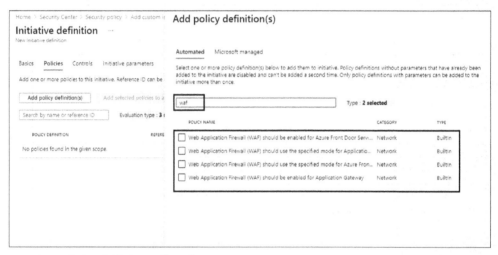

FIGURE 8-4 Custom initiative configuration

By clicking the + icon next to each recommendation, you can have these definitions added to your custom initiative, which will let these recommendations surface in your recommendations view for centralized monitoring. In addition to the built-in definitions, you also have the capability to add custom policy definitions.

Custom policy definitions

Although Microsoft includes many policy rules by default, there are times when you may want to create your own policy definitions. Policies are a core Azure capability and useful outside of Security Center. However, Security Center can leverage policies for compliance reporting, which is what you most care about. To get started creating your custom policy definition, you need to go to the **Policy** service in the Azure portal, navigate to the **Definitions** blade, and select "**+ Policy definition**" (see Figure 8-5).

FIGURE 8-5 Custom policy definitions

Although we won't be diving deep into policy creation in this chapter, be aware that there are three major parts of a policy definition:

- **Properties**   This is where you dictate the name, description, and category of the policy.
- **Parameters**   This is where you specify any variables that need to be used in the next step.
- **PolicyRule**   This is where you specify the resource type for the policy, and what field(s) to be checked for compliance.

> **TIP**   For more information on authoring custom policies go to *aka.ms/ AzNSBook/PolicyDefinitions*.

> **TIP**   If you are not comfortable or familiar with authoring Azure policies, there are security professionals both inside and outside of Microsoft who have authored policy samples and made them available publicly in various Github repositories.

Let's create a custom policy that is designed to turn on diagnostic logging for Azure Firewall instances:

1. In your browser, navigate to *https://aka.ms/AzNSBook/EnableDiagnosticLogs*; then click the **Deploy To Azure** button, as shown in Figure 8-6. This takes you to the deployment wizard.

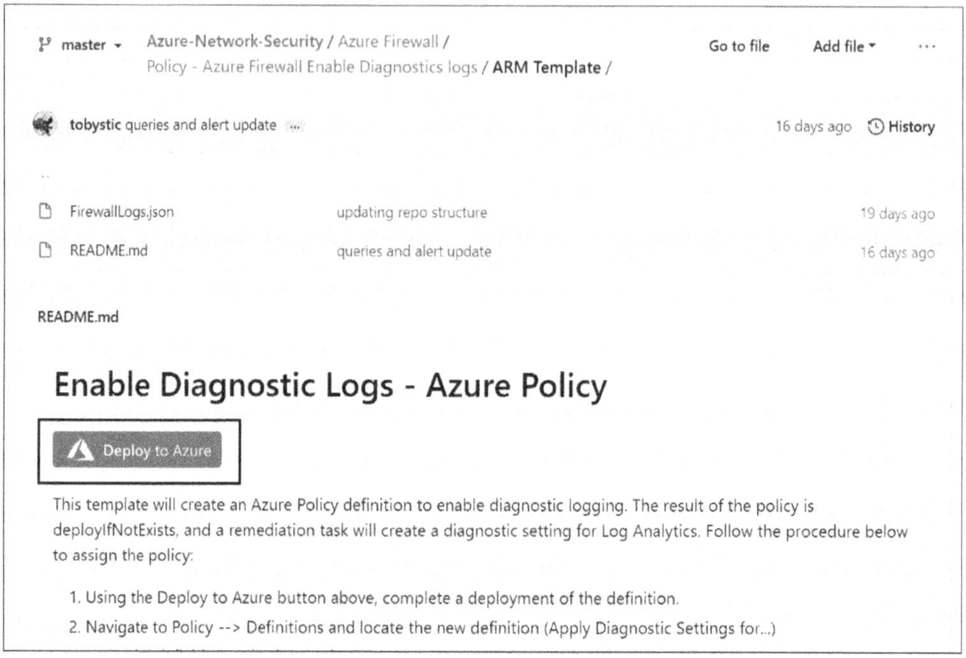

Enable Diagnostic Logs - Azure Policy

⚠ Deploy to Azure

This template will create an Azure Policy definition to enable diagnostic logging. The result of the policy is deployIfNotExists, and a remediation task will create a diagnostic setting for Log Analytics. Follow the procedure below to assign the policy:

1. Using the Deploy to Azure button above, complete a deployment of the definition.
2. Navigate to Policy --> Definitions and locate the new definition (Apply Diagnostic Settings for...)

FIGURE 8-6 Custom policies in Github

2. Choose your appropriate subscription and deployment region through the provided wizard. Once completed, the new policy will be available to be added to a custom initiative in Security Center and subsequently monitored as a new recommendation.

3. Back in Security Center, navigate to the Security Policy page and select **Add A Custom Initiative** at the bottom of the page; then click **+ Create New**. We'll name our initiative **Diagnostic Checks** and find the policy we just created by searching for "firewall."

4. Look for **Apply Diagnostic Settings For Microsoft.Network/azureFirewalls To A Log Analytics Workspace** and click the **+ button**.

5. As shown in Figure 8-7, you see some settings in the lower left that determine the options when fixing the recommendation. Fill out the settings as appropriate but ensure that **Enable Logs** is set to **True**.

6. Once you have verified your settings, click **Save**.

7. Add the new Diagnostic Checks initiative to the Security Center policy. Search for "diagnostic" and click the **Add** button next to the Diagnostic Checks initiative to open a wizard to finish the creation steps.

This process of adding policies to custom initiatives helps ensure you are monitoring what is important to your business. The default recommendations in Security Center, while broadly applicable, may not be in complete alignment with your business need. Adding policies for NSG configurations, firewall rules, and much more is critical to maintaining strong network security in the long run.

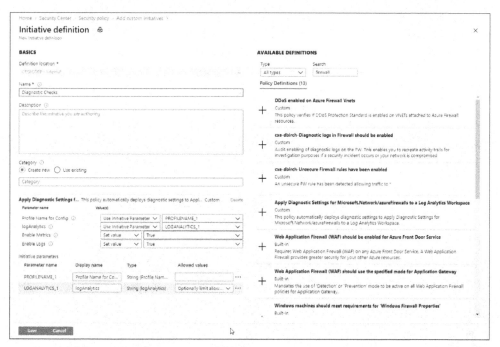

FIGURE 8-7 Adding a new policy to a custom initiative

Azure Defender

Azure Defender is the CWPP from Microsoft and can be found within the Security Center service in Azure. Although Azure Defender has "Azure" in the name, it extends its security capabilities to both on-premise and hybrid cloud environments. The core functionality of this service is to detect attacks and vulnerabilities and highlight them in the form of security alerts. In addition to alerts, there is a wide variety of other advanced capabilities including just-in-time VM access, adaptive network hardening, SQL/VM vulnerability assessments, and much more.

For network security, Azure Defender has a rich set of detections aimed at identifying myriad network-based attacks such as

- Possible SQL brute force attacks
- Possible outbound DDoS attacks
- Network communication with a malicious machine
- Suspicious outgoing SSH network activity

Currently, there are also two built-in detections for Azure DDoS, which highlight DDoS attacks detected and mitigated on public IPs.

> **TIP** To see the full list of detections, visit
> *https://aka.ms/AzNSBook/AzDefenderNetworkAlerts*.

In addition to security alerts, Azure Defender offers alert incidents. These are collections of alerts that have been fused together using Cloud Smart Alert Correlation—a system that makes use of AI combined with embedded security domain knowledge to intelligently correlate alerts with high fidelity and low false positive rates, drastically reducing Security Operations Center (SOC) alert fatigue.

One of the newer capabilities of Azure Defender is the Alerts map, shown in Figure 8-8, which is currently in public preview. This is an interactive global map that geographically represents the sources of attacks highlighted in your security alerts. Each dot is color coded according to severity and sized by attack frequency. You can select any dot to drill further into the alert itself to identify affected resources.

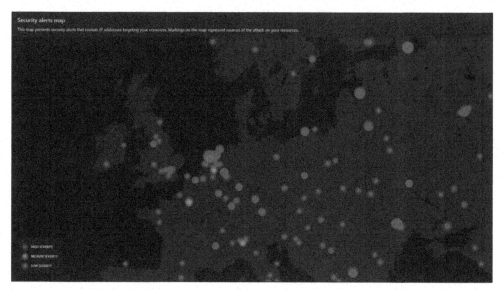

FIGURE 8-8 Azure Defender Alerts map

Azure Sentinel

Azure Sentinel is Microsoft's cloud-native security Information and event management (SIEM) solution with security orchestration automated response (SOAR) capabilities launched earlier this year and is designed to give you centralized incident management, investigation, dashboarding, and automated remediation capabilities all in one place. It should come as no surprise that a key cornerstone to network security monitoring would involve the use of a SIEM, and Microsoft's Azure Sentinel solution makes it easy to get started.

Although Security Center is useful for setting policies and recommendations that help you maintain a strong security posture, Azure Sentinel is the perfect tool for monitoring and responding to anomalous events, attacks, and potential compromise. We cover connecting your log data to Azure Sentinel so you can make use of the service's capabilities, working with incidents, using workbooks for visualizing your data, and using playbooks for automation. We conclude with the advanced hunting capabilities for proactive monitoring.

Data connectors for network security

In Chapter 7, "Enabling network security log collection," we cover how to set up diagnostic logging to a Log Analytics workspace which, for Azure network security products, is the primary requirement for a connector to show as enabled within Azure Sentinel. To see the list of available connectors, navigate to the Azure Sentinel service and choose **Data Connectors** from the navigation list, as shown in Figure 8-9.

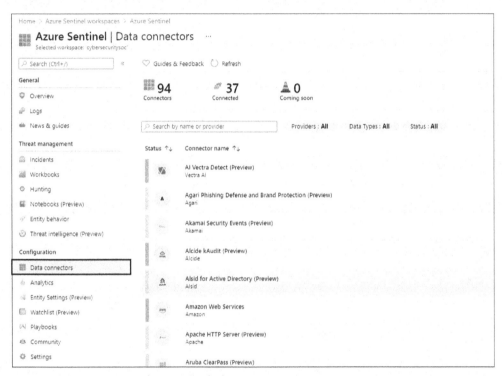

FIGURE 8-9 Data connectors in Azure Sentinel

It should be noted that there are several data connectors made available to you free of charge with 90-day retention. These are Office 365, Azure Activity Logs, Microsoft Threat Protection (MTP) alerts, and Azure Security Center alerts. Additionally, although it's not free, Azure Active Directory is a very useful data source because it contains sign-in logs. This is a valuable dataset if your organization uses Azure AD for single sign-on.

We focus on integrating Azure DDoS Protection, Azure Firewall, and Azure Web Application Firewall (WAF) (see Figure 8-10). All that you need for enabling a connector is to have diagnostic logs sent to Log Analytics, which was covered in the previous chapter.

FIGURE 8-10 Azure Web Application Firewall (WAF) connector

When you click a connector in the list, you see some additional information on the right. Make sure to look at the bottom-right corner in the Data Types section. These data types represent the data necessary for the connector to show as Connected. For example, Azure Web Application Firewall has three data types listed:

- AzureDiagnostics (Application Gateways)
- AzureDiagnostics (Front Doors)
- AzureDiagnostics (CDN)

In our environment, we are not currently logging CDN diagnostic logs, but we are capturing both WAF and Front Door logs, and that is plenty to start working with Azure Sentinel. Take a moment to review WAF, Firewall, and DDoS connectors and ensure you have the connectors showing in a Connected state, meaning you have diagnostic logging enabled.

Analytic rules and incidents

Now that you have verified that your Azure network security products are logging appropriately and that Azure Sentinel has enabled connectors, you can start looking at analytic rules and incidents. Incidents are created from enabled rules, and rules can either be created from rule templates or you can manually create your own rules based on a KQL query. First, look at the built-in rule templates by navigating to the rule templates page. Go to **Analytics** in the navigation bar and select the **Rule Templates** tab, shown in Figure 8-11.

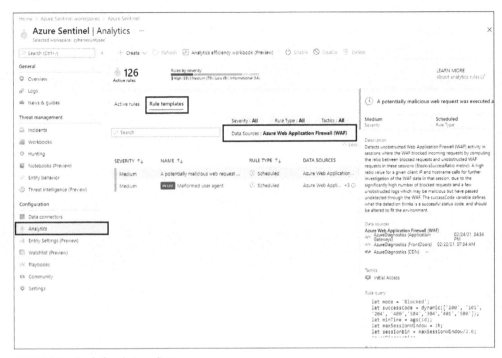

FIGURE 8-11 Analytic rule templates

As of the time of writing, the only Azure network security product that has built-in rule templates is Azure Web Application Firewall (WAF) and is focused on highlighting detections of malformed user agents. This analytic rule looks for instances where the user agent string used during communication appears suspicious. This can be a valuable indicator of attack because malformed user agents are often found hard-coded in malicious traffic.

Next to this rule, you can see the rule type is set to **Scheduled**. Most rules have this type, and it means that there is a KQL query that runs on a schedule, and if the rule thresholds are met, it creates an incident. The other available Rule Types are Microsoft Security, Fusion, and ML Behavior Analytics as detailed here:

- **Microsoft Security** This is a built-in-only rule type that creates incidents based on alerts that are triggered in connected security products.

- **Fusion** These are built-in-only rules primarily focused on detecting anomalous sign-ins followed by anomalous activity within Office 365. There are also a small number of fusion detections based on looking at related anomalous events found in both Palo Alto Networks firewalls and Microsoft Defender Advanced Threat Protection.

- **ML Behavior Analytics** These detections use built-in machine learning to look for anomalous events found in a number of various log types. Usually these are looking for statistically significant deviations from baseline data, such as a country that doesn't frequently log in or unusual IP addresses.

To turn a rule template into an enabled rule, select the rule from the **Rule Templates** tab, shown in Figure 8-12, and click **Create Rule** in the details pane on the right. Note that in the details pane you can view the underlying KQL query as well as the frequency the query is run.

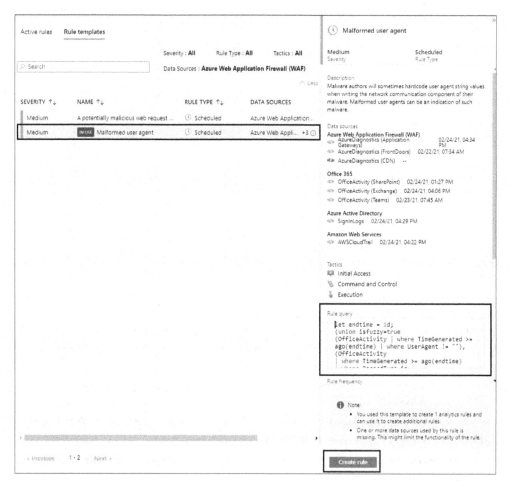

FIGURE 8-12 Azure WAF rule template

Because we said that currently we have rule templates only for Azure Application Gateway (WAF), let's see how we can enable custom rules for products like Azure Firewall and Azure DDoS.

Custom Rules

Although the provided rule templates are extremely useful for deriving quick value from Azure Sentinel, the flexibility of being able to create your own rules is useful for addressing specific use cases your organization might have. At the time of writing, both Azure DDoS and Azure Firewall can trigger incidents only from custom rules.

Rules created in Azure Sentinel make use of the Kusto Query Language (KQL) to return results from your data stored in Log Analytics. If results are returned, this would then create an incident, or multiple incidents, based on thresholds you set. These thresholds could be as low as "create one incident for each result from the query," or you may decide that you only want an incident to trigger if you see more than five results for a specific user. A good example would be failed logins that can be captured in the Azure Active Directory Sign-In logs. Triggering an incident every time a user fails to log in would be very noisy, but an incident firing if you see 20 failed logins over a 30-second period for a specific user could be an indicator of a brute force attack.

Luckily, if you are brand-new to KQL, you do not have to stress about being able to create custom rules. Sample detections have been created by security professionals both inside and outside of Microsoft and stored in various public Github repositories.

> **TIP** Find the Azure Sentinel Github repository at
> *https://aka.ms/ AzNSBook/AzureSentinelRepo.*

Workbooks

Workbooks are the primary visualization and monitoring tool within Azure Sentinel. If you are familiar with Azure Monitor Workbooks, this feature is an implementation of those workbooks, just with some slight differences. There are two categories of workbooks in Azure Sentinel: built-in workbooks and custom workbooks.

When using workbooks, you can either leverage the built-in workbook templates (shown in Figure 8-13) as is, customize a workbook template to meet specific needs, or create a brand-new workbook.

In Figure 8-13, the major components of the workbooks menu are

- **Workbooks and workbook templates** If you see a green bar to the left of the workbook, the workbook has been created.
- **Orange bar** The workbook template has received an update, and you can click the **Update** button in the lower-right corner to update the graphics and logic powering the workbook.
- **Prerequisites for using a particular workbook** Found on the right, they show you necessary data types and connectors.

FIGURE 8-13 Workbook templates

When you are working with a new template, you can first view the template to make any necessary edits, or simply click the **Save** button to start using the default template. At any time, you can delete any created workbooks by clicking the **Delete** button. This will not remove the template itself—just the workbook.

Let's create a workbook from the **Microsoft Web Application Gateway (WAF) – Azure WAF** template. If you are currently not using Microsoft Application Gateway (WAF) in Azure, you can choose a different workbook template. When you are ready, click **Save** and choose where to save the workbook. Once saved, click **View Saved Workbook**.

When you are first setting up the workbook, you likely will not have any rendered visuals because the template is not sure what you want to monitor. Choose to monitor all WAFs, and you should see your visuals render. If you chose a different workbook, you may have different options.

Any workbook can be customized—even those built from templates. To begin editing a workbook, click the **Edit** button in the upper left. You can tell you are in edit mode when each of the visuals has an Edit button next to it. Click the **Edit** button next to the WAF Actions pie chart. You should see a view like what is shown in Figure 8-14.

We will edit this visual to show only blocked and detected actions, as well as show the data over time on a line chart. Figure 8-15 shows the key areas that will change.

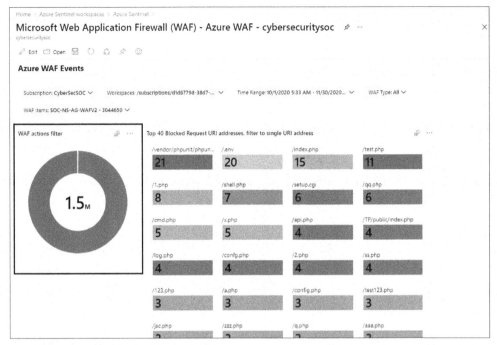

FIGURE 8-14 WAF workbook

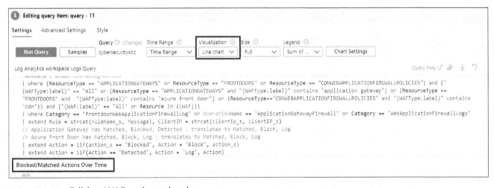

FIGURE 8-15 Editing WAF actions visual

1. In the **Advanced Settings** tab, change the visualization title to **Blocked/Detected Actions Over Time**.

2. Return to the **Settings** tab. Change the **Visualization** from **Pie Chart** to **Line Chart**.

3. At this point, you shouldn't be able to see your chart because our query does not return any timestamps for the visual to render on the x-axis. To fix this, on the last line of the query add **, bin(TimeGenerated, 1d)**. Remember to include the leading comma, which means that the data will now be summarized by both the action type, and the

timestamp. The **bin** function says to group together the data points for a given day so you can see aggregations across each 24-hour period.

4. When you are done making the changes, choose **Done Editing**, and you will see your new visual embedded in the workbook, as shown in Figure 8-16.

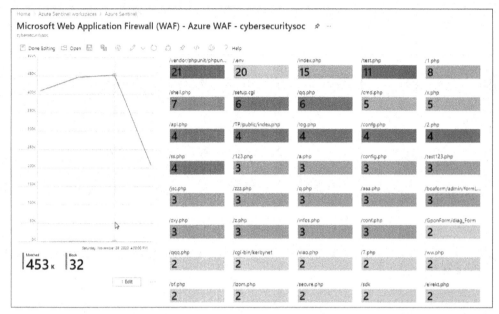

FIGURE 8-16 Edited WAF actions visual

At this point, you should see the power and flexibility available to you within workbooks. If you are concerned about picking up the KQL, don't be. It is one of the most accessible query languages I have ever seen, and by spending some time looking at and editing workbook visuals, you should quickly start to feel more comfortable.

> **TIP** Be sure to check out the KQL From Scratch course on Pluralsight, located at *https://aka.ms/KQLFromScratch*, which will give you a solid foundation in query design.
>
> Additionally, the Azure Data Explorer KQL Cheat Sheet (*https://aka.ms/AzNSBook/KQLCheatSheet*) and the SQL to KQL Cheat Sheet (*https://aka.ms/AzNSBook/SQLtoKQL*) are two great pieces of reference material.

Playbooks

Whereas workbooks are well designed for data visualization and effective monitoring of your network data, playbooks are designed for automating how you respond to incidents. When incidents are triggered in Azure Sentinel, the first logical step is to look at the incident, evaluate the potential impact, then decide what actions to take in response. Playbooks let you design reusable response logic that can be invoked both manually or automatically.

Some common scenarios carried out with playbooks are sending automated emails, opening support tickets, isolating compromised network assets, revoking user access for compromised credentials, and even making automated updates to firewall rules. The flexibility of the playbook ecosystem is so vast that the only limit to what can be automated is your imagination. If there isn't a built-in action you need, you can call Azure functions that run custom code in C#, Java, JavaScript, Python, and even PowerShell. The generic HTTP Web Request action is also very useful for making standard web API calls.

Playbooks are nothing more than Azure Logic Apps that are set to trigger an incident created in Azure Sentinel. There is a special trigger called When A Response To An Azure Sentinel Alert Is Triggered, shown in Figure 8-17.

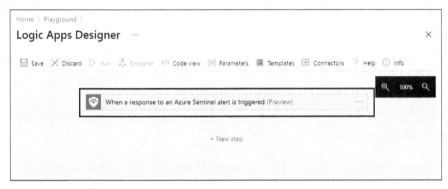

FIGURE 8-17 Playbook trigger

The trigger, when run, pulls a collection of information from the incident in JSON format and passes this into the subsequent actions under a value called Entities. The data stored here will be useful in subsequent steps. Using the Parse JSON action, as shown in Figure 8-18, is particularly useful in playbooks because it allows you to turn the JSON data into a set of reusable variables.

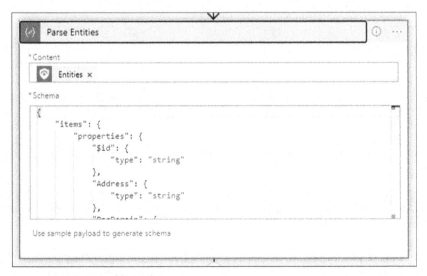

FIGURE 8-18 Parse entities action

There are many playbook examples available in the Azure Sentinel Github repository, and the process for leveraging them is simple. You can click the **Deploy To Azure** button (see Figure 8-19) on any provided sample to add the Logic App.

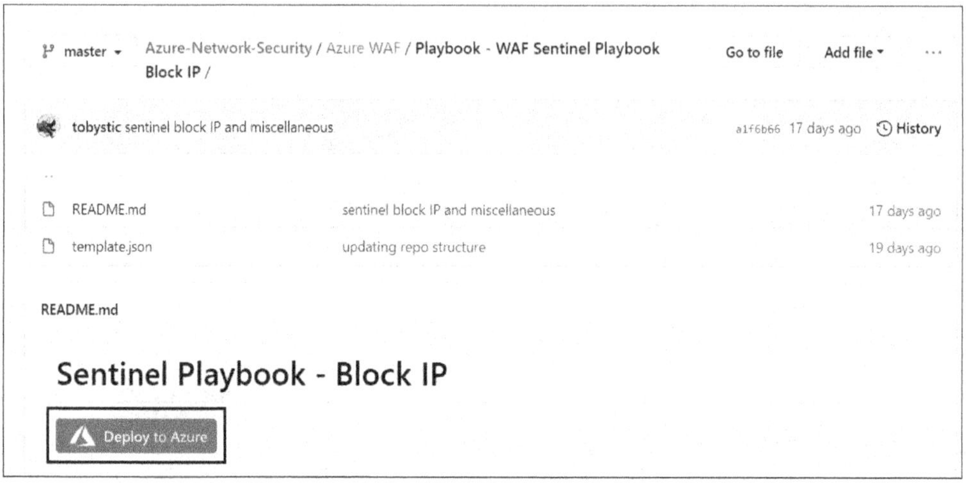

FIGURE 8-19 Deploy playbooks to Azure

Once the Logic App has been added, you may have to do some configuration of the Logic App's managed identity permission scope to ensure it has the appropriate permissions to execute the necessary steps. For more information, check out *https://aka.ms/PlaybookManagedIdentities*.

Once the playbook is configured, you can set it to run automatically in the **Automated Response** settings for an analytic rule, as shown in Figure 8-20. Every time an incident is triggered from this analytic rule, the provisioned playbook automatically runs the defined remediation steps, saving you and your SOC team enormous amounts of precious time.

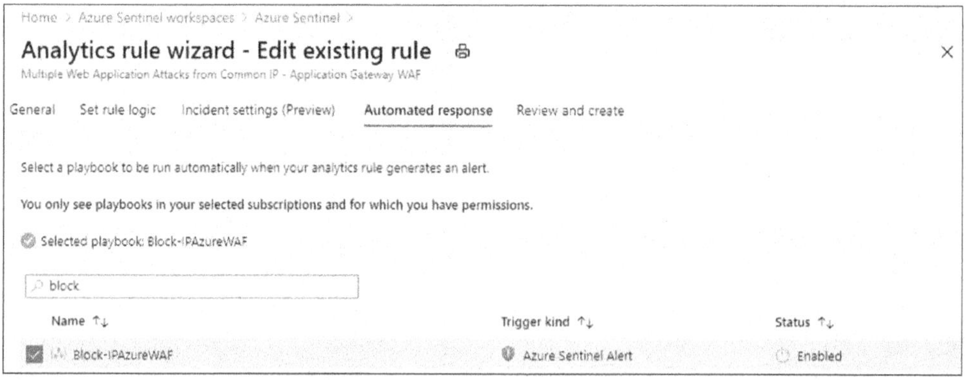

FIGURE 8-20 Automated Response settings

There are times where you may not want a particular playbook to run automatically—especially playbooks that take harsh actions against users, make configuration changes to network resources, or adjustments to network rules. As shown in Figure 8-21, you can trigger a playbook to run manually on a particular incident by looking at the full details of an incident and choosing **View Playbooks** on the right side of the alert record. Simply search for the appropriate playbook and click **Run**.

FIGURE 8-21 Run playbooks manually

Playbooks are an incredibly useful tool for any SOC analyst looking to easily handle routine responses to alerts, and they provide the flexibility to enact more aggressive responses when appropriate. Be sure to check the Azure Sentinel Github repository for community-created playbooks to accelerate your Azure Sentinel onboarding experience.

Hunting

We aren't diving too deeply into hunting in this chapter, but you should be aware of the value it provides when it comes to monitoring your network. Hunting allows you to set up reusable KQL queries that can either be run on demand or set up as a live stream. The overall goal of the Hunting tool is to allow SOC analysts to create queries that assist with investigating anomalies that you may not want to trigger incidents every time they are detected.

Live stream mode, shown in Figure 8-22, is a useful tool that allows you to monitor your logs for specific values, such as a compromised user, a malicious IP address, or any at-risk resource on your network.

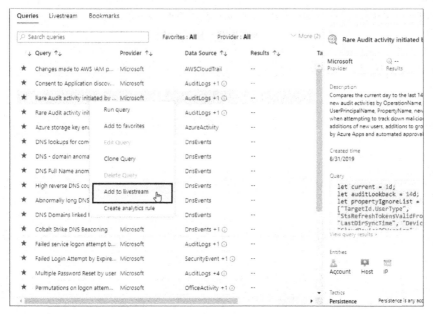

FIGURE 8-22 Add To Live Stream option

When you land on the Hunting page (see Figure 8-23), you can run all your queries at once and if you see any results you know what needs investigating.

> **TIP** Check out the community repository of Hunting Queries at
> *https://github.com/Azure/Orion.*

FIGURE 8-23 Hunting

Have a look at the Azure Sentinel Github repository for community-provided hunting queries, and feel free to contribute your own.

Network Watcher

While the primary focus of this chapter is around leveraging Security Center and Azure Sentinel for monitoring and remediation, it is worth taking a brief look at Network Watcher. Network Watcher offers the user a way to view network topology, investigate traffic flow issues both inside the network and to external locations, monitor network performance, and much more.

We're touching on two of these capabilities: topology and traffic flow verify. These tools help you both visualize your network configuration and validate connectivity of networked resources. Additionally, we will highlight the network map capabilities available in Security Center as it pairs nicely with Network Watcher's topology map.

Topology

Within the Network Watcher service, there is a section called Topology (shown in Figure 8-24) where you can view your existing network map as well as associated NICs and vNets. This is a standard network topology map and can be useful for gaining an understanding of how resources are connected and for architectural considerations of your various networks.

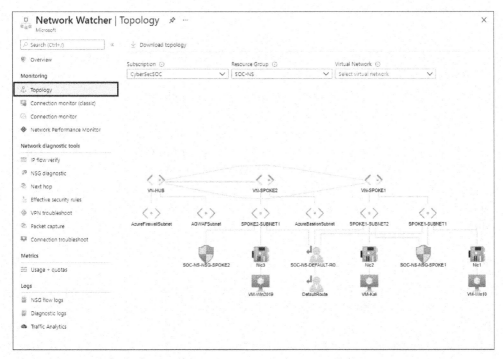

FIGURE 8-24 Network Watcher Topology

As shown in Figure 8-25, Security Center also has a version of the network topology map, but in a slightly different form and aimed at highlighting security risks.

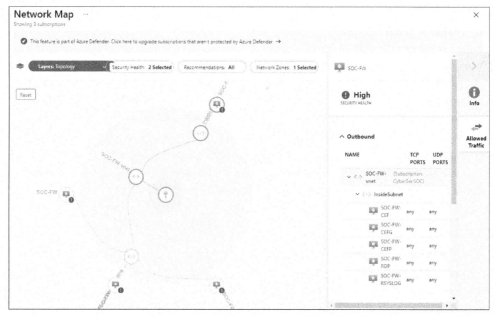

FIGURE 8-25 Security Center network map

This capability is part of Azure Defender, and you can find it by going to the Azure Defender blade and selecting Network Map. By default, you will be looking at just the network topology, but there are two interesting capabilities to be aware of:

- By checking the Allowed Traffic option, you can see a modified network map to view those resources that can talk to each other.

- Network Map may show you icons next to resources that denote any security risks on those resources, and you can filter the network map to show only resources that are of a specific risk. For example, the red exclamation point means high risk.

By using the network map with Allowed Traffic selected, you have a great way to see your at-risk resources and what other resources may also be at risk based on their communication paths.

IP Flow Verify

IP Flow Verify, shown in Figure 8-26, lets you check whether a specific resource on your network can communicate with another resource, both on and off the network, on a specified port.

For example, we are testing whether one of our Azure VM's can communicate on port 443 with Google's DNS server (8.8.8.8). When communication is successful, you see the green

Access Allowed message. Alternatively, this can be useful for verifying that communication is blocked between specific resources or ports to ensure isolation where appropriate.

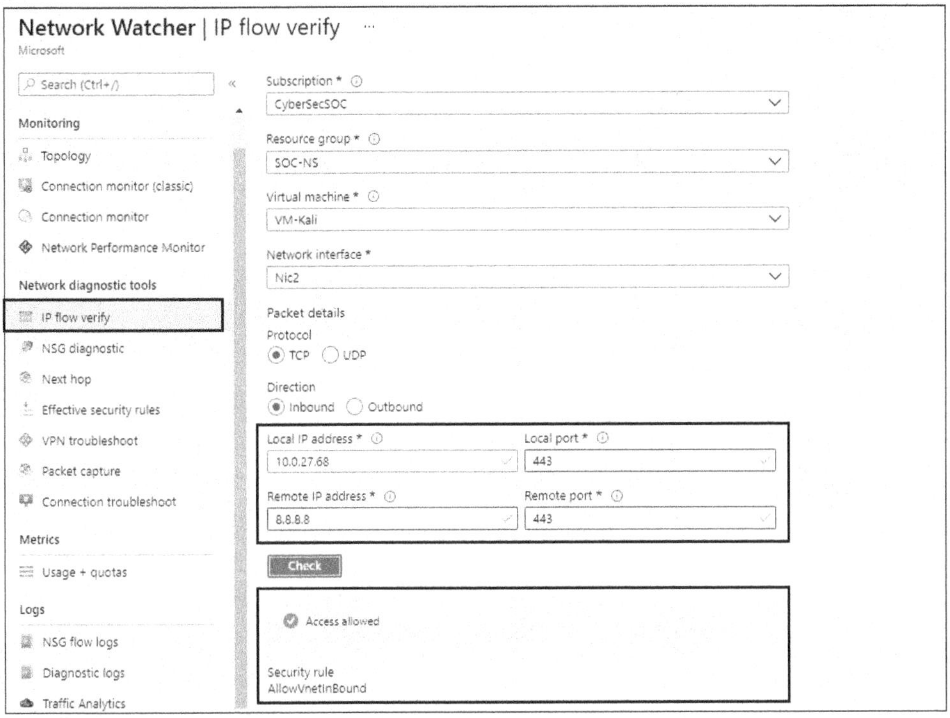

FIGURE 8-26 Network Watcher IP Flow Verify

Summary

Let us recap what we just covered. In this chapter, we touched on a lot of capabilities for monitoring and visualizing your network security data, and for most concepts we only scratched the surface of what is possible in Azure's network security monitoring, detection, and prevention toolset.

Security Center offers an easy way for IT operations and the SOC to jointly monitor networked resources to ensure a strong security posture of both existing assets and newly onboarded assets. Azure Defender is Microsoft's CWPP solution and sports advanced network layer detections as well as incidents, which are intelligently fused alerts to aid in reducing SOC alert fatigue.

We then moved into Azure Sentinel—Microsoft's cloud-native SIEM solution. By enabling diagnostic logging of your network security resources, you can take advantage of Azure Sentinel's connectors, which will let you use analytic rules to trigger incidents. These incidents can be configured to run remediation workflows automatically through the form of playbooks. Additionally, the hunting capabilities let you design reusable queries to carry out investigations and perform proactive anomaly searching. Finally, we covered some of the core capabilities of Network Watcher, where you can view the topology map of your network and test connectivity.

Knowing what is available to you is half the battle. The next step is to start implementing these capabilities into your own environments and build some processes around how best to monitor your own data. Even better is to bring your own expertise to the rest of the community by contributing to the Github repositories with your own queries, playbooks, workbooks, and ARM templates.

## Chapter 9

Combining Azure resources for a wholistic network security strategy

This chapter focuses on best practices to build and maintain a secure architecture design as environment complexity increases. Many deployments start with a small scope and gradually get added to over time, and it is important to ensure that changes and additions to the environment are made in a way that security is either maintained or improved.

The examples presented in the chapter start with the most basic virtual machine deployment and gradually build in complexity to include all the resources covered so far in this book and more. Each Azure environment is different, and with hybrid designs, the variety increases further. Each example is intended to be a starting point and a conceptual guide to build these examples into real-world scenarios.

Simple virtual network design

The most common scenario when transitioning to Azure is an Infrastructure as a Service (IaaS)–based approach that mimics traditional on-premise datacenter architecture, commonly referred to as "lift and shift." This architecture is a good starting point for the discussion that follows because it takes concepts familiar to any security professional and applies cloud-based controls.

The example starts with two virtual networks, each containing virtual machines that serve different purposes. See Figure 9-1 for the diagram of the most basic configuration to be discussed. In this example, the primary network security topic is restricting traffic to and from the VMs in each network.

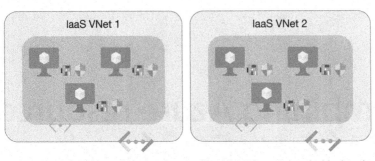

FIGURE 9-1 Two independent virtual networks with NSGs associated with virtual machine network interfaces

Virtual network isolation

In this example, there are two virtual networks, and we assume those networks are in the same Azure tenant and subscription. Even if the networks use nonoverlapping IP address ranges within the same network class (10.0.10.0/24 and 10.0.20.0/24, for example), the virtual machines within each network would not have connectivity to the machines in the other VNet.

The concept of VNet isolation is important in secure network design because simply provisioning resources in separate networks can be a very effective method of creating a boundary between resources. Unless VNets are peered together, there is no way to communicate between separate virtual networks. If peering is necessary, the IP addresses used must be nonoverlapping.

Another benefit of creating multiple virtual networks to isolate resources is that IP addresses can be reused to conserve address space. If there are environments that do not need to be part of a larger network, which is increasingly common in cloud networks, any private IP address range can be used without having to consider the broader IP address management strategy. Of course, if connectivity to the larger network is necessary, especially to on-premise networks, then IP address conservation will be important, which makes planning more complex.

Network security groups

In the simple IaaS example, network security groups (NSGs) are depicted as being attached to the network interfaces of each virtual machine, but they could alternatively be associated with the subnets. An NSG-only model like this can be effective to segment networks, but as networks grow more complex and the resource count increases, NSG management can become prohibitively difficult to manage.

East-west traffic is probably the easiest to manage with NSGs because all NSG rules are IP address based. Using NSGs for segmenting traffic within subnets or within VNets is a common practice, even in more complex networks where central traffic management is handled by Azure Firewall or an NVA.

NSGs become less effective as the sole traffic management mechanism when it becomes necessary to control inbound or outbound traffic. Inbound traffic should be centralized to purpose-built ingress points, such as Application Gateway, Load Balancer, or Azure Firewall. Outbound traffic is also difficult to manage with NSGs because of the inability to create rules for FQDNs. For these reasons, NSGs should be considered a supplementary solution that are only to be used on their own in very small or test environments.

Hub-and-spoke topology

The most common advanced network architecture in Azure is the hub-and-spoke topology. The purpose of this architecture is to centralize the management and security of network controls in a hub virtual network. Figure 9-2 depicts one way the simple IaaS VNets from the previous example could be integrated with a hub. This example has Azure Firewall deployed in the hub network to control traffic to and from each network.

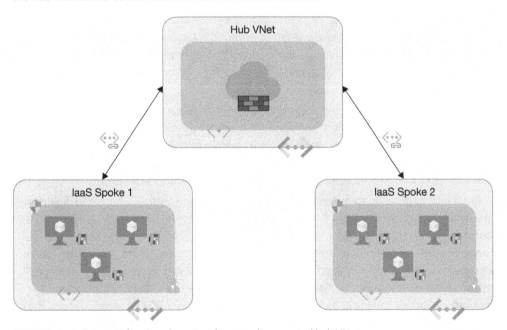

FIGURE 9-2   A diagram of IaaS spoke networks peered to a central hub VNet

VNet peering

As discussed previously, virtual networks are isolated from one another by default, providing a built-in security boundary. To create a hub and spoke topology, virtual network isolation must be bypassed by creating peering relationships between networks. From a security standpoint, there are some considerations to make so that peering networks does not amount to the same result as having one large, flat network.

When peering networks, the direction must be set, and the administrator should consider the need before automatically creating a bidirectional peering. If the operation of resources on the networks does not truly require bidirectional traffic flow, then peering can be configured to allow traffic to flow only in one direction.

In the example architecture pictured previously, using Azure Firewall as the central security inspection point, peering relationships do not need to be created between every virtual network. If all networks were peered and traffic could flow freely between any of them, this would be a mesh topology, and the design would defeat the purpose of central management and security. In the hub-and-spoke model, peering is only created from each spoke to and/or from the hub, and never from spoke to spoke. This ensures that any traffic that leaves a VNet passes through the Firewall for inspection.

Routing

Peered VNets enable traffic to leave one network bound for another, but further configuration is necessary to direct traffic to the right destination. Routing can be a very important security boundary because traffic is simply unable to flow to a given destination if a route to that destination is not present.

To make the hub and spoke topology function, routes passing traffic to the Firewall must be added to every subnet that contains resources that will use this traffic path. Not all resources need to access resources in other VNets, but most require internet access of some sort, which is best managed centrally. For this reason, most or all subnets in a hub-and-spoke topology need routes assigned that direct traffic to the Azure Firewall in the hub virtual network.

Another consideration to make when deciding how to route traffic is whether to direct only inter-VNet traffic to Azure Firewall (traffic leaving the source VNet) or to route subnet-to-subnet inter-VNet traffic to Azure Firewall as well. By default, traffic within the same VNet will be able to reach other destinations within that same VNet. However, if the appropriate routes are configured, traffic between two subnets in the same VNet can be routed to Azure Firewall instead of being passed directly. The benefit of this configuration is that any traffic control decisions are made centrally at the Firewall without the need for NSGs between subnets. The primary drawback of routing in this way is the increase in the complexity (number of hops) of the traffic path.

Hybrid Access

In scenarios where connectivity is required between Azure networks and on-premise networks, the link can be established using VPN or ExpressRoute. Once set up, there are some architectural options that have an impact on network security.

Some organizations choose not to allow any traffic to leave Azure directly, and instead send traffic back to on-premise networks for inspection. This is an architecture that becomes less common as time progresses. This can be achieved using simple routing or by using the Azure Firewall Forced Tunneling feature (which also relies on routing). Using Azure Firewall for this purpose allows Firewall to control all east-west traffic in Azure, then hand off outbound traffic to a central inspection pipeline.

Virtual WAN is an option to consider when hybrid connectivity is required. One way to use VWAN Secured Virtual Hubs is somewhat of a reversal of the previous example of forcing traffic back on-premise. With Secured Virtual Hubs, traffic from either on-premises or Azure virtual networks is passed to the VWAN hub and inspected either by Azure Firewall or a partner solution.

Integrating PaaS services

By default, most PaaS services are only able to be accessed over the public internet. For some compliance frameworks, this is not considered an acceptable risk, even if the traffic is encrypted and the service is behind authentication. Luckily, there are options available to prevent broad access to PaaS resources.

If PaaS services can remain accessible over the public internet, there are steps that can be taken to secure both the source and destination by restricting traffic. If a virtual machine needs to access an Azure SQL instance, this should not automatically cause all outbound traffic to be allowed from that VM. To prevent command and control or data exfiltration by a compromised machine, traffic should only be allowed to specific destinations. In this case, you can use an Azure Firewall Network Rule to allow traffic to the SQL service tag. On the destination side, the PaaS resource firewall should be used to restrict access to only known sources whenever possible.

In scenarios where private network communication is required, you can use Azure Private Link to inject a PaaS service into a virtual network and assign it a private IP address. This ensures that the resource is not accessible over the internet at all and all communication is done over private networks. Read more on Private Link at *https://aka.ms/AzNSBook/ PrivateLink*.

In Figure 9-3, the ongoing example topology is expanded to include a third spoke VNet, which contains Private Endpoints for both SQL and Storage PaaS services. Integrating these services into the existing hub-and-spoke provides private connectivity to the PaaS services from resources in the IaaS networks, provided the correct routes and firewall rules are in place.

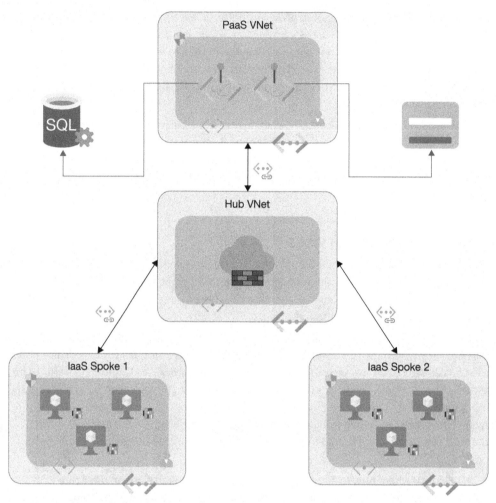

FIGURE 9-3 The same hub-and-spoke configuration with the addition of a third spoke VNet that contains Private Endpoints for PaaS services

Secure administrative access

For IaaS workloads in Azure, some option must exist for machines to be accessed for administration, whether that is hypervisor administration via the Azure portal or remote access to the operating system via command line or graphical interface. Securing all methods of access is a vital part of any Azure security strategy.

Remote access

When virtual machines are provisioned in Azure, the default option is to attach a public IP address. Many customers choose to allow inbound communication to this public IP address on remote management ports such as 22 and 3389. Anyone who has looked at access logs to observe the constancy of brute force login attempts to public resources would agree that having VM management ports exposed to the internet is risky.

Azure Firewall provides one method to centralize remote access to machines throughout the network using Destination NAT rules. Using DNAT rules, each VM is able to have only a private IP address, and Azure Firewall listens externally for traffic on one of its associated public IP addresses, often on nonstandard ports. Although this centralizes the open ports to one IP address, it does not reduce the total number of ports available for inbound traffic. Security by obscurity is not really security.

Azure Security Center offers Just-in-Time (JIT) VM access, which can apply to either VMs with public IP addresses or can integrate with Azure Firewall. With JIT enabled, management ports are always closed unless an authorized user requests access to the machine for a period of time. Upon requesting access, temporary rules are created using either NSG or Azure Firewall DNAT. This approach greatly reduces the attack surface by reducing the time that ports are exposed. Learn more about JIT at *https://aka.ms/AzNSBook/JIT*.

To fully remove direct public access to VM management ports, you can use Azure Bastion to provide a remote management experience only available via authenticated access to the Azure portal. Bastion does expose a public IP address, but that address cannot be used to connect directly to the resources in the VNet where it exists. Instead, all remote access goes through a web browser via the Azure portal.

As shown in Figure 9-4, a Bastion subnet has been added to one of the IaaS spokes from the example. In this configuration, an administrator needs to access the Azure portal first to connect to machines in the network. This access is subject to RBAC in Azure (authorization) as well as the controls available in Azure Active Directory (authentication), including MFA and Conditional Access. Once connected to Bastion, it is now possible to connect to VMs in other VNets via peering.

Role-based access control (RBAC)

Access to the Azure portal is extremely important as part of any Azure security strategy. The network security tools that are the focus of this book are themselves Azure resources, and the management layer must be secured. Both authentication and authorization must be set up properly to contribute to a secure environment.

When designing an access strategy in Azure, multifactor authentication (MFA) should be considered a requirement. At a time when many people use MFA to access their social media accounts, there is no reason not to enforce MFA on Azure portal access, especially because there's no extra cost to implement MFA in Azure.

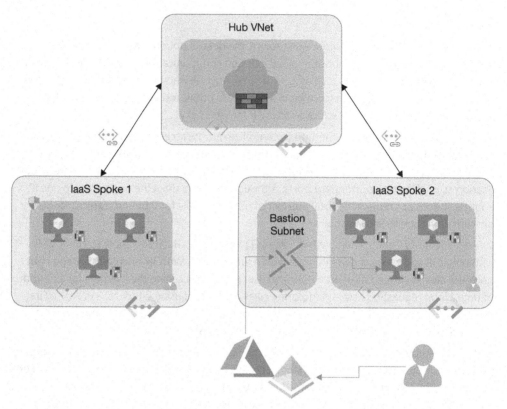

FIGURE 9-4 Two spoke VNets peered to a central hub with Azure Bastion in one spoke network

Once signed in to Azure, architects should pay attention to what resources any accounts have access to read and change. One relevant example of using RBAC to separate resource access is using Firewall policies to abstract settings away from the firewall itself to enable a separation of duties; one role can edit the Firewall, and another can edit the policy.

Application design scenarios

Web applications hosted in Azure can take on many forms, largely dependent upon the architecture the components reside within. This section reviews some example application architectures and the security implications associated with each.

Security controls need to exist at every step in the process of application delivery, from the application code all the way to the point the content is served to the user. When determining the application architecture, security must be a primary factor because every technology and design choice throughout the stack influences security.

An example that illustrates the importance of application architecture in determining the security of an application stack is the choice of load balancers. There is guidance published at *https://aka.ms/AzNSBook/LoadBalancing* that details the considerations to make when choosing a load balancing strategy. It is important to keep in mind that even if application delivery requirements are fulfilled by a particular tool, it may not be the case that security is also sufficiently addressed. For instance, while a Load Balancer could potentially fill the regional load balancing role behind a Front Door, there is no mechanism present to verify application information to ensure traffic is coming from the desired entry point.

Application Gateway behind Front Door

Azure Front Door with WAF serves as a highly capable and secure ingress point for applications hosted in Azure and elsewhere, and there are many back-end options for Front Door. Any public endpoint can be added as a back end for Azure Front Door, but it is most common to put Front Door in front of other Azure resources.

Starting from end users accessing an application, the first point of entry to the application environment is also the beginning of the security stack. When Front Door is the initial ingress point, a WAF Policy should be attached to the Front Door to block any attacks as early as possible. Behind the Front Door, Load Balancer or Application Gateway could be used to distribute traffic within each region. In this instance, Application Gateway is the more capable tool because it has both the ability to make application layer routing decisions and the ability to add additional security options.

Figure 9-5 adds the secure application delivery components to the example network design. The hub VNet has been expanded to include a subnet for Application Gateway with WAF, and Front Door with WAF is in front of the Application Gateway's public IP address. In this example, the web application is served by the machines in the IaaS network, which use PaaS services as a data layer. The traffic path a user request takes starts with Front Door as traffic is inspected by WAF and sent to the Application Gateway, which performs an additional check as discussed in the next section. Application Gateway is configured to route any internal traffic to Azure Firewall, which sends it to the VMs in the IaaS network. As the VMs make calls to their back-end SQL and Storage components, these calls are routed to the PaaS network through Azure Firewall. Azure DDoS Protection Standard is enabled on the hub network to provide additional assurance that any potential attack will be mitigated.

Application Gateway with WAF can be used to ensure that traffic forwarded to it originates from trusted sources and has been previously inspected. Using an NSG on the Application Gateway subnet is a good method to lock down traffic from specific sources. However, because Azure Front Door is a multitenant service, permitting the Front Door Service Tag only ensures that traffic originates from Front Door, not necessarily a specific one. This introduces the risk, however slight, that a malicious actor could provision their own Front Door to pass traffic to back ends and bypass WAF inspection. Fortunately, Front Door appends every request with a header value, X-Azure-FDID, which is unique to each instance. Using Application Gateway WAF, a custom rule can be created, as shown in Figure 9-6, to deny any traffic that does not contain the header.

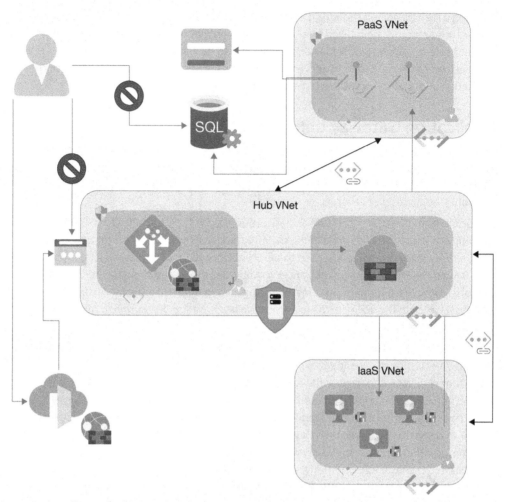

FIGURE 9-5 The previous hub-and-spoke topology with IaaS and PaaS VNets with expansion to include secure application delivery components

Another benefit of using Application Gateway with WAF as the regional application load balancer behind Azure Front Door's global footprint is the ability to serve applications, or portions thereof, only to private networks. When this is required, the same Application Gateway that is serving public content to Azure Front Door can also publish a private application to an internal listener. In this configuration, public and private applications are able to share infrastructure while remaining separate. It is important to use WAF to inspect application traffic even on private networks, and this design allows for that inspection.

FIGURE 9-6 A screenshot of a custom WAF rule to verify the X-Azure-FDID header

Azure Kubernetes application

Applications hosted using AKS have the advantage of being able to use the built-in functionality of Application Gateway as a Kubernetes ingress controller. WAF policies can be applied to the Application Gateway Ingress Controller (AGIC) for Kubernetes in the same manner as they would be in a standard Application Gateway. To learn more about the configuration of AGIC, see *https://aka.ms/AzNSBook/AKS*.

An AKS environment, like any other compute environment, may require outbound communication that must also be secured. Traffic can be routed to Azure Firewall to inspect and direct traffic leaving the AKS cluster. Use the following link for detailed documentation about securing AKS outbound traffic with Azure Firewall: *https://aka.ms/AsNSBook/AKSEgress*.

Firewall or WAF?

Some organizations have historically limited the number of ingress points to networks in an attempt to reduce attack surface. To this end, it is a common requirement to have all traffic, ingress and egress, pass through some firewall appliance. This can be an effective strategy, but sometimes there is good reason to forgo an extra control or extra hop when there is no tangible benefit. As with any security and technology decision, whether to use a single common ingress point should be a decision based on costs and benefits. Some guidelines can be found at *https://aka.ms/AzNSBook/Firewall-WAF*.

Azure Firewall Premium can terminate TLS connections, giving it application layer visibility. However, this inspection is not offered for inbound connections. Azure Firewall is a service that is effective primarily for network layer traffic control and inspection. Ideally Azure Firewall should be deployed outside the application delivery stack, and services like Application Gateway and Front Door should handle application traffic separately from the traffic path of Firewall.

Application Gateway can sit in front of Azure Firewall, forwarding traffic to application back ends through Firewall. This design carries the benefit of centralized traffic logging using Azure Firewall, as well as the ability to use Firewall's DNS configuration to resolve internal FQDNs. In this configuration, Azure Firewall would not be aware of the original source IP of the requests, so it would not be able to apply Threat Intelligence to requests. This issue is partially mitigated if Bot Mitigation rulesets are enabled on WAF.

Azure Firewall could also be deployed in front of WAF. The only possible benefits of this design are the conservation of public IP addresses and the application of a larger TI database than what bot mitigation uses. Overall, the costs tend to outweigh the benefits in this scenario because the original source IP is hidden from the Application Gateway and WAF.

Network Security Monitoring

As detailed in Chapter 7, "Enabling network security log collection," all relevant security data from Azure network security tools can be forwarded to central repositories and analyzed using some of the techniques in Chapter 8, "Security monitoring with Azure Sentinel, Security Center, and Network Watcher." If security is a priority, then data should be collected from every service mentioned in this book. Ideally, resource data should be collected from every resource in Azure and anywhere else.

Data collection strategy

In some environments, data collection is decentralized and only enabled and used by the teams directly responsible for the operations of resources. This is effective for operational troubleshooting but could leave gaps for security.

For the best visibility, there should be a central data collection and analysis strategy. In Azure, this could take the form of a single central Log Analytics workspace with Azure Sentinel enabled, and every relevant resource logging to the workspace. This centralization gives security teams the advantage of being able to analyze data across a large environment rather than looking at narrow pockets of data.

Taking a summary of the components that have been part of the example network topology until now, Figure 9-7 shows the relevant data collection points and their destinations. PaaS services should have diagnostic logs enabled, as well as use Azure Defender for threat detection, when applicable. Data from diagnostic logs go to the central Log Analytics workspace, whereas Azure Defender threat detection alerts are forwarded to Security Center, which can be forwarded to Azure Sentinel. Every other resource in the environment should also be configured to forward diagnostic logs to the central workspace, along with the platform-level Azure Activity logs. NSG flow logs need to be fed to Network Watcher Traffic Analytics for the resultant data to be written to the workspace. Azure Sentinel, when added to the workspace, will have visibility into any action performed.

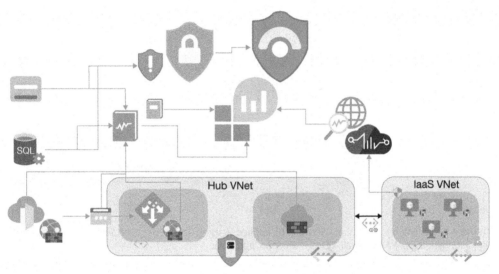

FIGURE 9-7 A modified version of the hub-and-spoke model showing the sources and destination of security data

Cloud secure posture management

Much of the focus of security monitoring tends to center around the events that occur in an environment, represented by logs of various kinds. This sort of visibility is often that which detects malicious activity and hopefully leads to the prevention of harm.

Configuration monitoring and management is in many ways the governing force around what activities are possible at all. If a resource is configured securely in the first place, then the risk of malicious activity is greatly reduced. For example, if responsible firewall rules are in place, then several steps in the kill chain are prevented.

Keeping resources in a securely configured state is a large task, and Azure has some purpose-built tools to accomplish it. See *https://aka.ms/AzNSBook/AzurePolicy* for an overview of using Azure Policy to detect and remediate common misconfigurations and use Security Center to visualize these policies, both built in and custom, to show an overall score of secure configuration: *https://aka.ms/AzNSBook/SecureScore*.

Figure 9-8 shows some examples of where Cloud Secure Posture Management (CSPM) principles can be applied. Security Center has many built-in policies as part of its default Azure Policy initiative, which apply to several of the topics covered in this chapter, and additional policies can be added to custom initiatives to import to Security Center. Potential targets for Security Center and Azure Policy include ensuring logging is enabled throughout the environment, verifying that WAF is enabled where applicable and configured in prevention mode, and making sure Azure DDoS Protection Standard applies to every critical public workload where it applies.

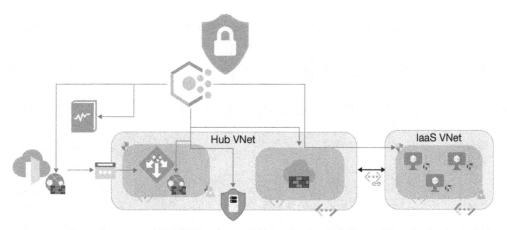

FIGURE 9-8 Several resources that CSPM can be applied to using Azure Policy and Security Center, including diagnostic logs, WAF, Firewall, DDoS Protection, and NSGs

Summary

This chapter has covered several architectural design concepts that help to create the best possible security posture in Azure. Network designs start simple but always become more complex over time. Each addition of complexity introduces new security challenges. To solve these challenges, many examples have been presented to segment, protect, and monitor your Azure networks.

Throughout this book, many strategies and tools have been introduced so that each contributes to an effective network security strategy. These strategies apply to a wide variety of Azure resources. In summary, some points to remember are

- Apply the principles of Defense in Depth and Least Privilege to network traffic.
- Think about network security as part of architectural design.

- Secure networks control traffic in every direction.
- Data is the currency of security detection and response, and network tools should be positioned and configured to generate as much good data as possible.

It is our hope that you are now more equipped to secure Layers 3, 4, and 7 in your Azure deployments.

Index

Hear about it first.

Since 1984, Microsoft Press has helped IT professionals, developers, and home office users advance their technical skills and knowledge with books and learning resources.

Sign up today to deliver exclusive offers directly to your inbox.

- New products and announcements

- Free sample chapters

- Special promotions and discounts

- ... and more!

MicrosoftPressStore.com/newsletters

Plug into learning at

MicrosoftPressStore.com

The Microsoft Press Store by Pearson offers:

- Free U.S. shipping

- Buy an eBook, get three formats – Includes PDF, EPUB, and MOBI to use with your computer, tablet, and mobile devices

- Print & eBook Best Value Packs

- eBook Deal of the Week – Save up to 50% on featured title

- Newsletter – Be the first to hear about new releases, announcements, special offers, and more

- Register your book – Find companion files, errata, and product updates, plus receive a special coupon* to save on your next purchase

 Pearson